THE
CONSPIRACY
TO END
AMERICA

ALSO BY STUART STEVENS

It Was All a Lie:
How the Republican Party Became Donald Trump

The Innocent Have Nothing to Fear:
A Novel

The Last Season:
A Father, a Son, and a Lifetime of College Football

The Big Enchilada:
Campaign Adventures with the Cockeyed Optimists from Texas Who
Won the Biggest Prize in Politics

Feeding Frenzy:
Across Europe in Search of the Perfect Meal

Scorched Earth:
A Political Love Story

Malaria Dreams:
An African Adventure

Night Train to Turkistan:
Modern Adventures Along China's Ancient Silk Road

THE CONSPIRACY TO END AMERICA

FIVE WAYS MY OLD PARTY IS DRIVING
OUR DEMOCRACY TO AUTOCRACY

STUART STEVENS

12

TWELVE

New York   Boston

Twelve
Hachette Book Group
1290 Avenue of the Americas, New York, NY 10104
twelvebooks.com
twitter.com/twelvebooks

First Edition: October 2023

Twelve is an imprint of Grand Central Publishing. The Twelve name and logo are trademarks of Hachette Book Group, Inc.

The publisher is not responsible for websites (or their content) that are not owned by the publisher.

The Hachette Speakers Bureau provides a wide range of authors for speaking events. To find out more, go to hachettespeakersbureau.com or email HachetteSpeakers@hbgusa.com.

Twelve books may be purchased in bulk for business, educational, or promotional use. For information, please contact your local bookseller or the Hachette Book Group Special Markets Department at special.markets@hbgusa.com.

Library of Congress Control Number: 2023942124

ISBNs: 978-1-5387-6540-1 (hardcover), 978-1-5387-6541-8 (ebook)

Printed in the United States of America

LAKE

10 9 8 7 6 5 4 3 2 1

For Ukraine;
at a time when many Americans seem to take democracy for
granted, Ukraine reminds us of the price

Contents

A Massive Fraud of this type and magnitude allows for the termination of all rules, regulations, and articles, even those found in the Constitution.

—*Donald J. Trump, 45th President of the United States*

The Conspiracy to End America

I remember the moment clearly. I was watching the sun come up in Park City, Utah, where I'd been working with the Lincoln Project to defeat Donald Trump. It was a couple of weeks before the 2020 election and it had been another all-nighter, one of many during that campaign in my personal war against Donald Trump and the modern Republican Party I had helped create. I'd just finished one of the over three hundred videos we frantically produced in just a few months, and I was tracking the latest polling from the handful of key states: Pennsylvania, Wisconsin, Michigan, Arizona, Nevada.

This was the sixth presidential campaign I'd worked on, and I felt like I had spent half my life locked in rooms working the numbers in those same states. I had helped elect governors or senators in all of them and could discern the patterns developing in the often confusing and contradictory flow of data. In that instant, the fog of political war lifted, and I could see the outcome with confident clarity. Donald Trump was going to lose. Joe Biden would be the next president of the United States.

I sent off my latest video and fell asleep, allowing myself to think about life after Trump. As a media consultant who had helped elect more Republicans to top office than any in my tribe, I felt a deep personal responsibility for what the party had become. After the 2016 election, that burden drove me to write *It Was All a Lie: How the Republican Party Became Donald Trump*. But that morning before the 2020 election, I felt that my duty had been done. I had fought as hard as I could and used every bit of my skills to blow up the Death Star of Trump. I could not change my past. My political memory would always play in the key of regret. But I was free to move on.

Had you asked me that morning if Republicans would accept defeat if Joe Biden won by over 8 million votes and north of 300 electoral college votes, my answer would have been simple: What else could they do? They wouldn't like it, but when you walk off the field of the Super Bowl, the score is the score. Endless hours would be spent by the despondent losing fans analyzing what could have been done differently, but none of it would matter. The final scoreboard was never wrong.

I should have known better. Any faint hope I had that the Republican Party might seize on a Trump defeat as an impetus to self-correct was quickly destroyed. I watched Republican senators and congressmen I'd help elect, men and women I knew to be sane and decent, refuse to acknowledge what grade-school children knew to be true: Donald Trump had lost the 2020 race. When I spoke to a few, I heard variations of "We're just humoring him. What harm can it do?"

Soon their answer would come as they ran for their lives from domestic terrorists their leader had called to action and their complicity had emboldened.

The greatest danger is often not recognizing the greatest danger. The need I experienced before the 2020 election to believe there was a salvageable normal in American politics was as predictable as it was dangerous. But today's Republican Party is not a "normal" political party in the American tradition. It has become an autocratic movement masquerading as a political party. If we look away from that truth, we greatly increase the likelihood that the America we love will slip away, never to return.

Whenever a democracy slides into autocracy, there are five critical elements at work. All of these are active today in American politics. The tendency is to examine each as if it is an isolated phenomenon, troubling perhaps but manageable by the American system. This illusion is the hope of the autocrats and a potentially fatal mistake. Each of these is part of a greater whole that together threatens the existence of the American experiment. This book is an urgent warning to examine collectively the power of the forces working together to end American democracy as we know it.

The five autocratic building blocks are:

- Propagandists
- Support of a major party
- Financers
- Legal theories to legitimize actions
- Shock troops

This is the conspiracy to end America. All are growing in power and influence as their cumulative impact metastasizes more dangerously every day. Fox News is a small part of an entire ecosphere of media that looks to autocrats like Viktor Orbán of Hungary as their role models. American oligarchs like Peter Thiel, who has openly voiced his opposition to democracy, combine with a vast online base of small donors to provide virtually unlimited funding for their cause. The Republican Party refuses to admit that America has a legally elected president. After the coup attempt of January 6, Republicans in forty-seven states introduced legislation to change voting laws, the product of a quiet, right-wing legal industry that has been at work for decades methodically altering the legal framework of democracy. The insurrectionists who stormed the Capitol are now heroes and martyrs to a fierce network of men and women who believe they have a moral obligation to remove the current illegal occupant of the White House. Donald Trump has summoned them to fight "the final battle." They are answering the call.

This is not theoretical for me. I know many of these people, know their world and how they function. As dangerous as they may seem, they are worse.

This is testimony to a corrupt system I helped construct, a book I never would have imagined writing in my years as a Republican political consultant. Now it is a book I can't imagine not writing.

It is not too late to save American democracy. But it is too late to pretend that the danger is not great, and the time grows short.

Chapter 1

The Propagandists

Those who manipulate this unseen mechanism of society constitute an invisible government which is the true ruling power of our country.

—*Edward Bernays,* Propaganda *(1928)*

I fell into political media consulting by chance. I was in film school at UCLA and got a call from the chief of staff of a congressman I'd worked for as a page when I was in high school. That congressman, Thad Cochran, was now running for the Senate and his chief of staff, Jon Hinson, had decided to run for his congressional seat. His Democratic opponent was the son of powerful Mississippi Senator John Stennis and it seemed everyone expected him to win easily. "I don't have any money to hire anybody to make commercials," Hinson told me. "So you have to do it."

I told him that was interesting, but I didn't know how to make commercials. "I just make these stupid little films," I told him. But Hinson was desperate, and I had always loved politics, so I finally agreed to give it a try. Hinson ended up winning an upset, mostly because he was in the right place at the right time, and to my great surprise, I discovered people would pay me to make commercials. I could do it sort of seasonally like migrant labor work, I presumed, taking a few months to work in campaigns while I tried to find a way into the film and writing world.

Early in his second term, Hinson would resign from Congress when he was arrested having sex with another male in a bathroom on the then little-used sixth floor of the Longworth House Office Building. When I later discovered the odd and seemingly contradictory reality that many conservative Republicans are gay, it seemed less surprising that my first client had so ended his brief career.

Even though Hinson didn't last long in Congress, his win was considered a rare uphill landslide, and it launched my career. The secret to success as a political consultant is to work for people who are going to win anyway and just not screw it up. I was lucky to work for good candidates, and by 1988—a few political cycles later—my video work had found its way in front of Roger Ailes, and he liked it enough to hire me to make a film for the 1988 Republican National Convention. The film was scheduled to run just before the keynote speech and its theme was "Celebrating the American Dream." What that meant to Ailes and the Bush campaign was a film filled with profiles of demographically correct people who had gotten rich during the Reagan-Bush administration.

The centerpiece of the film was a female Vietnamese immigrant who had started a successful catering firm in law school that serviced United Airlines. It was a great story. We'd spent a lot of money and were deep into it when we learned she had also worked as a Playboy Bunny for extra money. "Two hundred and fifty million Americans and we can't find one who wasn't a Playboy Bunny?" the Bush pollster Bob Teeter incredulously asked Ailes.

"What's the problem?" Ailes shot back. "It makes it a better story."

As it turns out, no one had mentioned to the chosen keynote speaker, New Jersey Governor Tom Kean, that plans called for a film to run before his speech. He didn't like the idea and it died. But Ailes still wanted me to finish the film and said he'd be happy to personally buy airtime to run it. That was Roger. He did not like to lose arguments of any kind.

Four years later, the expectation was that Ailes would return as the Bush reelection campaign's director of media operations. This cycle, the pollster Robert Teeter was running the campaign, and for some reason—rumored to be his displeasure with the amount of money he would be paid—Ailes never returned in the same role. He continued to encourage me in politics, always glad to call prospective clients on my behalf. When he left consulting to run Fox News, I remember vividly a lunch in New York when he told me, "I want to call it Fair and Balanced." He repeated the tagline as if savoring a particularly tasty bite of his meal. "Fair and Balanced." Then he laughed and shook his head. "Pretty good, huh?"

There is a basic misunderstanding of the role of right-wing media in the creation of the modern Republican Party. The conventional wisdom is that Fox News is a great danger to democracy for what it has done to the Republican Party. "The most important conservative television news source in America is currently pandering to an extremist president," Tom Rosenstiel, director of the American Press Institute, said in an interview with *Vox*. "It's distorting the Republican Party. It's damaging the Republican Party. It's changing conservatism. Fox is making the news, not covering it. It's remaking the Republican Party, not informing its audience." That's understandable but it is far too benign a view of the Republican Party.

If you believe that perspective, you're convinced that one of the two major parties in the world's only superpower consists of millions of patriotic, well-intentioned Americans who were driven to abandon deeply held values by a cable channel that, at its peak, gets less than a third of the regular audience of *Storage Wars*. Before he was fired, the most-watched show on Fox was *Tucker Carlson Tonight*, which drew regular audiences of only about 3.5 million viewers. Did a single, marginally watched network drive the world's oldest democracy in a country of 318 million people to the greatest crisis of governing since 1860?

No, that's nonsense. It's akin to blaming the Afrikaner press for apartheid or the failure of the *Daily Worker* for America's rejection of communism. Fox News did not create the modern Republican Party. The Republican Party created Fox News.

Millions of Americans do not believe that Joe Biden is a legally elected president because of a network that has only twice the audience of HGTV. They believe it because the Republican Party embraced the lie, promoted the lie, and continues to assert the lie as its official position. Had every Republican elected official who knew that Joe Biden won a decisive victory taken the simple step of congratulating the president-elect of their country, it would have instantly isolated Donald Trump and Fox News and others would have fallen in line. The responsibility lies not with the paid propagandists and the cranks and scam artists in the media of the right. None of these people took an oath to uphold the Constitution. Had the Republican Party maintained even the pretense of being a moral, governing party, none of what happened after the 2020 election would have unfolded as it did.

The people running Fox News comprehend this, and although they logically promote their power as kingmakers, they understand that they are *servicing* a market, not creating it. They know their business model relies on following a political movement, not creating one. Fox News head Rupert Murdoch admitted as much when he agreed with a Dominion Voting Systems lawyer in his deposition in that company's libel lawsuit. "[The issue] is not red or blue, it is green."

In 2021, Fox News lost 29 percent of its total viewers

compared to 2020 because it didn't shout the election lie as loudly as its right-wing competitor Newsmax. Murdoch and Fox hosts knew without question the election claims they spouted were "crazy," but they worried that the facts would hurt the company's "stock price."

As the *Washington Post* wrote of the Dominion lawsuit, "The filing is rife with examples of Fox News hosts and executives worrying that departing from Trump's line, or questioning his team's claims, might hurt their business model. They worried especially about Newsmax, which was less discerning in its coverage of Trump's election conspiracy theories and saw a rating boom at the time."

For Ailes, the creation of Fox News was just an extension of what he did as a political consultant. And yes, what I did. Ours was a profession in which truth had no meaning. While there actually is a published code of ethics drafted by the American Association of Political Consultants, the first sentence is "I will not indulge in any activity which would corrupt or degrade the practice of political consulting." That makes the other nine points of the ten-point plan completely meaningless. What could you do to degrade a profession like political consulting?

There is nothing about the practice of political consulting that is related to truth, objectivity, and furthering the greater good. The ethical code of the Society of Professional Journalists reads like a list of *worst* practices for political consultants. Among them are guidelines encouraging reporters to:

- Take responsibility for the accuracy of your work. Verify information before releasing it. Use original sources whenever possible.
- Remember that neither speed nor format excuses inaccuracy.
- Provide context. Take special care not to misrepresent or oversimplify in promoting, previewing or summarizing a story.
- Never deliberately distort facts or context, including visual information.

Roger was never happier than when he was doing the *opposite* of all that. And while Ailes's storied history as a political consultant is well known, people seem to truly underappreciate how much Fox News utilized the basic tools of political consulting. For Roger, Fox News was his chance to create the Ultimate Republican Campaign.

When Fox News began broadcasting, it was a simple but brilliant play for television to dig into the market that conservative talk radio had been feasting on for decades. The target audience of viewers was clear. While it was useful for the network to appear interested in non-white Americans, it was widely understood—and accepted—that 90-plus percent of their viewers would be white. The concept of "truth" was useful only to the degree that it was persuasive—and disposable when it wasn't useful. "Everything Roger wanted to do when he started out in politics, he's now doing 24/7 with his network," says a former News Corp executive in a 2011 *Rolling Stone* piece by Tim Dickinson. "It's come full circle."

It's easy to say that Fox News and its spawn were just a conservative alternative to the liberal media. But that would make the mistake that William F. Buckley Jr. described when he wrote, "To say that we and the Soviet Union are to be compared is the equivalent of saying that the man who pushes the old lady into the way of an oncoming bus and the man who pushes [her] out of the way…are both people who push old ladies around."

None of the right-wing media outlets including Fox News ever intended to exist within the parameters of standard American journalism. To the extent that it was useful, they would insist they were "fair and balanced," as Ailes laughingly told me when he was launching Fox News. He directed the building of sets that looked like network news shows and hired a sprinkling of true journalists so he and his team could point to them, demanding that they should be treated like journalists. A very tough interviewer like Chris Wallace, solid reporters like Shep Smith and John Roberts, and a brilliant commentator like Charles Krauthammer enabled Fox News to erect a Potemkin village of serious intent.

Both Ailes and Fox News owner Rupert Murdoch would assert that there was a very distinct line between the network's news coverage and the shock-jock commentary of Bill O'Reilly and Sean Hannity. "We police those lines very carefully," Ailes insisted. I can picture Roger trying not to laugh as he said it. As *Rolling Stone*'s Tim Dickinson reported in 2010, Ailes employed John Moody, a former *Time* magazine reporter, to direct the coverage. "This is not 'What did he know and when did he know it?' stuff," Moody instructed the Fox newsroom in a memo during the September 11 congressional hearings. "Do not turn this into Watergate. Remember the fleeting sense of national unity that emerged from this tragedy. Let's not desecrate that."

Moody later was forced out of Fox News after writing a column attacking the U.S. Olympic Committee for celebrating diversity, accusing its members of wanting to "change the Olympic slogan to Darker, Gayer, Different." That was two years after Ailes, his protector, had been fired in 2016 for the sexual harassment he engaged in and encouraged at Fox News. Moody went on to partner with another ousted Fox News executive, Ken LaCorte, at LaCorte News, which was exposed for operating a series of troll websites intended to help elect Trump in 2016. The *New York Times* described it as "Russian Tactics"—the hiring of young Macedonians to create websites with names like Conservative Edition News to promote false conspiracy theories about Hillary Clinton, including her supposed ties to a pedophile ring.

When I worked for Republican candidates, we viewed Fox News and the right-wing ecosphere as an extension of our campaigns against Democrats. "Bill Clinton has 15,000 press secretaries," Ailes said in 1992, attacking reporters for their pro-Clinton bias. "At some point, even you guys will have to get embarrassed." Unburdened by journalistic standards, Fox News was free to operate using the classic tools of state-controlled media. Claiming that "Ukraine is full of Nazis" is a variation on "Democrats are the real racists." There were periods in American history in which that would have been a defensible statement. But to accuse the modern Democratic Party, which is supported by 90 percent of African Americans, as being "the real racists" is a lie expressed as an absurdity. In state propaganda, history and time are like LEGO blocks, to be arranged into whatever creation is most useful. In his 1946 essay "The Prevention of Literature," George Orwell described the process. "Totalitarianism demands, in fact, the continuous alteration of the past, and in the long run probably demands a disbelief in the very existence of objective truth."

This was and is the essential difference between the dominant "liberal" media institutions in the United States and the Fox News version of "news." Truth and facts do have a place in the *New York Times*, *Washington Post*, CNN,

MSNBC—the news media the right loves to hate the most. Propaganda views truth and facts as obstacles to be navigated, not values to be honored.

For decades, I spent more time than most sane people arguing with reporters and editors of the hated liberal press. I won some of those arguments, lost most, but it was a conversation based in reality and accepted truths. It was often frustrating, sometimes infuriating, but never did I feel like I was living in a world of "alternative facts."

In an essay for *The Bulwark*, long-time conservative writer Mona Charen describes the change that began when Barack Obama was elected:

> But then things went sideways. While we can't say the Fox News effect was entirely responsible—talk radio too played a role, as did social media—it started to become evident during the Obama years that the right's impatience with press bias had curdled into something more ominous. Instead of seeking to fact-check and balance coverage, Republican and conservative audiences demanded combat. Newt Gingrich turbocharged his anemic presidential campaign in 2011 by using the primary debates not as an opportunity to draw contrasts with his opponents but as a forum for attacking the press. When *Politico*'s John Harris asked Gingrich about a philosophical dispute

regarding health insurance, Gingrich wheeled on him. "I hope all of my friends up here are going to repudiate every effort of the news media to get Republicans to fight each other to protect Barack Obama, who deserves to be defeated, and all of us are committed as a team—whomever the nominee is—we are for defeating Barack Obama."

I was at that primary debate and watched the crowd vibrate with delight. But Gingrich didn't win the nomination; Mitt Romney won. During the primary, it was obvious that few in the right-wing media wanted Romney to be the nominee. There was a long list of preferred candidates—from then–Texas Governor Rick Perry to nutty as a fruit cake Newt Gingrich. Even former Pennsylvania Senator Rick Santorum was preferred by the Fox News crowd over Romney.

I found this particularly ironic. I was working in Pennsylvania Republican politics when the late Arlen Specter agreed to endorse Santorum in the 1994 Republican primary for the U.S. Senate if Santorum would agree to support him when he ran for the Republican presidential nomination in 1996. Specter was probably the most liberal Republican in the Senate, and adamantly pro-choice. Santorum, who based much of his political identity on his supposedly deep moral opposition to abortion, eagerly agreed to Specter's proposed deal. There is a video clip of him standing on stage applauding Specter's announcement—a bizarre event on the National Mall at which Roger Stone introduced Specter.

It's difficult to believe that the same party nominated Mitt Romney and, four years later, Donald Trump. But once Romney won the nomination, Fox News and the media on the right lined up to support him. From my position inside the Romney campaign, it was clear that there was a group of white low-propensity voters who could be motivated by racist attacks and xenophobia. This is a path Romney never would have condoned and it was never considered. But had Romney called for a Muslim ban as Trump did in December 2015, the right-wing media would have enthusiastically supported it. Had he called Mexicans coming to America "drug dealers, criminals, rapists," the right-wing media would have stood up and shouted their approval. When Romney lost to Obama by 5 million votes, had he refused to concede the election, as Trump did when he lost by over 7 million votes, Fox News would have stood by him just as they stood by Trump.

This is the dividing line between press sympathy for liberal Democrats and the conservative media's devolution into propaganda. Had John Kerry claimed the 2004 race was a fraud, no major media organization would have supported him. Had Barack Obama attacked Muslims and called for a religious ban, he would have been attacked by the same newspapers that endorsed him. And if he had done so, it is difficult to imagine Obama winning their endorsement.

As every government intelligence agency *and* the Republican-led Senate Intelligence Committee concluded, Russian intelligence assets worked to elect Trump in 2016. That success is surely one of the greatest covert-operation achievements in modern history. The Russians understood how the right-wing media world operated. Instead of having to influence and compromise reporters one by one, they were the recipients of the entire web of the Republican Party propaganda machinery when they helped elect a Republican president.

—————

Back in the 1930s, infamous Stalin apologist Walter Duranty of the *New York Times* was simply one reporter at one newspaper, albeit a critically influential one. Duranty's lies helped kill an untold number of innocent Ukrainians when he helped hide from the world the horror of Stalin's forced famine, the Holodomor. But Duranty, as evil and duplicitous as he was, did not aspire to undermine democracy in America.

Donald Trump held *precisely* that aspiration, and when he was elected, the Russians suddenly had a unique power base in American politics. The most reliable opponents to Russia and the Soviet Union—conservative Republicans—were now the leading pro-Putin faction in American politics. It's difficult to imagine that even the most optimistic Russian intelligence officer believed their covert operation could possibly be so successful. Despite the irrefutable conclusion that Russia attacked American democracy and helped elect Trump, much of the conservative media defended Russia by calling it a "Russian Hoax," employing only the thinnest pretense that a criminal collusion charge was not brought against Trump, so therefore the Russian influence did not exist.

Bizarre as it is to see those on the right defending a once-mortal enemy, MAGA America and Putin's Russia have developed a shared worldview. Historian Timothy Snyder divides nation-states into those with the underlying belief in "the politics of inevitability" in contrast to the bleak "politics of eternity." America and the Soviet Union were once the epitome of these differences.

Believing the myth of manifest destiny, Americans have long possessed an innate optimism, the conviction that they live in the greatest country in the history of the world, and it will always be such. Our problems and crises may be severe, but they are played out against the assumption that our national greatness was inevitable. Even Black Americans who had the greatest reason to abandon hope in the American experiment—those who had been enslaved, murdered, and tortured to stop them from participating in democracy, the actual victims of the failures of American society—have continued to hold faith in the inevitability of their progress.

In Russia, as in the Soviet Union, any hope for positive change has proven illusory. Instead, the leaders have cultivated a unifying identity as a nation of victims. To be Russian is to suffer. So, when you greatly suffer, you realize your greatness as a Russian. Do not expect your leaders to make your life better because this is your fate. "Whereas inevitability promises a better future for everyone," Snyder writes in his brilliant book *The Road to Unfreedom*, "eternity places one nation at the center of a cyclical story of victimhood." It is exactly that shared sense of victimhood that has defined the MAGA movement and driven the Republican Party toward autocracy. It reflects a complete collapse of the values that the Republican Party once espoused as foundational.

In Ronald Reagan's America, conservatives believed that to be born in the United States was to win life's lottery. "My fellow citizens, our nation is poised for greatness," Reagan intoned in his second inaugural speech. "Let history say of us, These were golden years—when the American Revolution was reborn, when freedom gained new life, when America reached for her best."

Reagan's America was scored in the key of hopeful inevitability. It was the America of World War II, not Vietnam. There would be challenges, difficult days, a Battle of the Bulge, and maybe even another Pearl Harbor, but there would always be V-E and V-J Days just over the horizon.

The Reagan optimism was defined by opposition to the bleak totalitarianism of the Soviet Union. With that belief came the certainty that the future belonged to America. Ronald Reagan standing in Berlin demanding "Mr.

Gorbachev, tear down this wall" was a demand that epitomized those core beliefs. When the Berlin Wall came down and the Iron Curtain lifted, those events proved the cause was just, the outcome inevitable.

Today, the demonization of immigrants is a constant of right-wing media. But for Reagan, immigrant America was the key to American greatness. He announced his 1980 general election campaign with the Statue of Liberty as a backdrop in a celebration of an America built by immigrants. "They came to make America work. They didn't ask what this country could do for them but what they could do to make this—this refuge—the greatest home of freedom in history. They brought with them courage, ambition, and the values of family, neighborhood, work, peace, and freedom. They all came from different lands, but they shared the same values, the same dream."

Reagan's final speech as president was another ode to immigration: "We lead the world because, unique among nations, we draw our people—our strength—from every country and every corner of the world. And by doing so we continuously renew and enrich our nation."

Twenty-eight years after Reagan left office, the majority of white conservatives believed they lived in a very different nation. In Donald Trump's world, to be an American was to be a victim of powerful forces, globalist conspiracies, and wealthier countries. "For many decades," Trump declared in his inaugural address, "we've enriched foreign industry at the expense of American industry, subsidized the armies of other countries while allowing for the very sad depletion of our military." Reagan's proud, strong America had been stolen, and replaced by a nation of chumps. "We've made other countries rich while the wealth, strength, and confidence of our country has dissipated over the horizon. The wealth of our middle class has been ripped from their homes and then redistributed all across the world," Trump roared from his inaugural podium.

"That was some weird shit," former President George W. Bush is reported to have quipped to his fellow former President Barack Obama following Trump's speech. And so it was for two American presidents of contrasting ideologies, Bush and Obama, who were united by the shared belief in what it meant to be American. But not Donald Trump and his nation of white victims. Trump was the only president in American history who delivered his inaugural address in a bad mood. Even on the day of what should have been his greatest triumph and a celebration of American democracy, Trump was angry, as if his own election proved how much America had been cheated.

Donald Trump's America was the home of the aggrieved, the bitter. Its guiding emotion was fear, unfocused and specific. Fear of the future, fear of non-whites, fear that being anything other than a serial heterosexual is contagious, fear of Big Tech. Trump's America meant living in a world with the knowledge that someone else is getting a break you aren't, that it doesn't matter how hard you work, there is no chance of betterment. Run as hard as you can, but the bastards will always dial the treadmill faster.

In the Republican view, the long trek from Ronald Reagan to Donald Trump traveled from a "shining city on the hill" to a dark and frightening place of "carnage." This dark vision of Trump's inaugural address was hailed by Fox News as "muscular," "masterful," "completely nonpartisan." Katie Pavlich, the editor of the right-wing website *Townhall*, praised it on Fox News, gushing, "It almost sounded like Abraham Lincoln when he talked about the government."

Electing Donald Trump was an act of grievance, a way to settle the score. For four years, he was the most powerful man in the world. For two years, his party controlled the House and the Senate. It was the perfect opportunity to stick it to the system, to finally right all the terrible wrongs people had suffered under eight years of a Black president. It was time to Make America Great Again.

———

Four years after that angry inaugural speech, Trump's indignation had escalated to a rage. He was the only outgoing president of the modern era not to appear at the inauguration of his successor. Once again, he wanted us to believe, America had been victimized, the office of the presidency stolen not solely from Trump, but from America. As Ruth Ben-Ghiat writes in *Strongmen: Mussolini to the Present*, "One final principle anchors the sweeping changes that come with an authoritarian rule: the leader's claim that he does not just represent the nation, as do democratic heads of state, but embodies it and bears its sorrows and dreams." Donald Trump was the Real America. And when the "Deep State" stole the presidency from him, it was stolen from the American people.

Trump accomplished very few of the goals he promised throughout his campaign and outlined in his dark inaugural speech. "Every decision on trade, on taxes, on immigration, on foreign affairs will be made to benefit American workers and American families," he had promised. "We must protect our borders from the ravages of other countries making our products, stealing our companies, and destroying our jobs. Protection will lead to great prosperity and strength."

Yet after four years in the White House, Trump left office with 3 million *fewer* Americans employed. He was the first president since Herbert Hoover to lose jobs on his watch. After telling *Washington Post* reporter Bob Woodward he could end the national debt "over a period of eight years" without tax increases, he increased the debt more than any non-wartime president in U.S. history. Trump's promises of protectionist policies saving the American economy ended with the trade deficit increasing from $481 billion to $679 billion.

When running for president, Trump had vowed to deport millions of undocumented workers, praising President

Eisenhower's infamous "Operation Wetback" deportation policy from the 1950s in a debate. "I like Ike," Trump bellowed. "Moved a million and a half illegal immigrants out of this country, moved them just beyond the border. They came back. Moved them again, beyond the border, they came back. Didn't like it. Moved them way south. They never came back. Dwight Eisenhower. You don't get nicer; you don't get friendlier."

In August 2019, *USA Today* published an analysis of the language Trump had deployed in his attacks on immigrants. "Trump has used the words 'predator,' 'invasion,' 'alien,' 'killer,' 'criminal,' and 'animal' at his rallies while discussing immigration more than 500 times," *USA Today* tallied. "Trump has used [the phrase] 'get the hell out of our country' at least 43 times during his rallies."

But after four years, the rate of deportation had fallen over 50 percent lower under Trump than Obama. When his predecessor left office, 542,411 cases of deportation were pending in courts. By the time Trump slumped out of the White House, that number had risen to 1,290,766.

Yet none of this mattered. When Trump said he "could shoot somebody on Fifth Avenue and nobody would care," he was right. He understood his voters. As president, he didn't shoot anybody, but his incompetence, mendacity, and general stupidity killed millions, at a time when the ravages of COVID demanded presidential leadership. And none of

Trump's voters—the surviving ones at least—cared. Voting for Trump had nothing to do with solving problems. That was that thing called "governing," which involved "policy," and that wasn't why MAGA voters loved Trump. They embraced Trump for how he made them *feel*. On Fox News, Pete Hegseth defended the anger of the tiki-torch white protestors at the 2017 "Unite the Right" rally in Charlottesville, describing their motivation as "I feel like my country is slipping away. And just because I talk about nationalism—not white nationalism—doesn't mean I'm talking in code, that I'm a racist."

For Trump voters, his failures only confirmed that his voters had been right in their fervent support of him. His inability to deliver on his promises proved how much the system was stacked against them. If Donald Trump couldn't do it, nobody could. Trump's failures weren't an indictment of Donald Trump but rather an indictment of democracy.

"I just think that the reason why we're so susceptible to autocracy now is that we're no longer telling ourselves this positive story of the nation," historian and author Peniel Joseph told NPR in an interview in 2022. "And I think Trump was brilliant in this way. He [sold us a] very divisive, anxiety- and fear-riddled view of the nation-state."

Donald Trump's election proved that the majority of self-described conservatives had abandoned a belief in the inevitability of America. "I don't want to sit around and tell my kids stories about how great America used to be," Fox

News host Laura Ingraham told the crowd in her speech at the 2016 Republican National Convention. Democracy was not the crown jewel of the America they loved. Democracy had become the instrument of the *destruction* of the nation they loved. Trump ran as a xenophobic racist, and once the Republican Party embraced him as their leader, it legitimized threads of extremist conspiracies that had previously been limited to the ecosphere of the far right.

When Trump announced his candidacy for president with attacks on Mexicans as rapists and drug dealers, he was immediately endorsed by Andrew Anglin, the founder of the neo-Nazi website *The Daily Stormer*: "I urge all readers of this site to do whatever they can to make Donald Trump president." Anglin later predicted accurately: "If The Donald gets the nomination, he will almost certainly beat Hillary, as White men such as you and I go out and vote for the first time in our lives for the one man who actually represents our interests."

J. M. Berger, a fellow at the International Centre for Counter-Terrorism at The Hague and George Washington University's Program on Extremism, wrote an essay for *Politico* shortly before the 2016 election examining Trump's appeal to the white nationalist movement:

The convergence of white nationalists around a mainstream candidate marks a major development in the post-Civil Rights Act era of American politics. While they have opposed Democrats actively in past elections, their attitudes toward Republican candidates largely have been ambivalent, with many opting out of politics altogether. Now, with Trump, that has changed, raising the prospect that the nominee of a major political party is tapping a deep well of anti-Semitism and racial hate—intentionally or unintentionally—and is mainstreaming such views in the process. If Trump wins the election, subscribers to those views believe, they will be able to claim increased legitimacy and seek a bigger role in mainstream politics.

Which is exactly what happened. Conspiracies blaming the federal government for plots against white people have fueled the white nationalist movement for decades. It was a constant on the radio programs of William Cooper, whom President Clinton is reported to have called the "most dangerous man in America," as well as the race war novel *The Turner Diaries* by William Pierce. After Trump's election, these wack-job conspiracies moved out of the shadows into prime time. "The Democratic Party has decided that rather than convince you, people who are born here, that their policies are helping you and making the country better and stronger," Tucker Carlson warned on his now canceled Fox News show, "they will change the electorate." Tucker spread the "Great Replacement Theory" that non-whites were being brought to the United States to reduce the power of white Americans. The *New York Times* reported that Carlson "amplified the idea that Democratic politicians and others want to force demographic change through immigration" during more than four hundred episodes of his show, devoting more than *fifty* hours to that single theme. This was no longer a nutty idea printed in pamphlets given out at gun shows; it was now being treated like a serious policy debate. "The long-term agenda of refugee resettlement is to bring in future Democratic voters... to change the racial mix of the country," Carlson said as if he were discussing the impact of higher taxes on the economy.

On May 14, 2022, an eighteen-year-old white male walked into a Tops grocery store in a predominately Black neighborhood of Buffalo, New York, and murdered ten people, wounding three others. All but two were Black. The shooter left a 180-page "manifesto" that made it clear the Great Replacement Strategy was his motivation. He threatened all non-whites and wrote that they should leave "while you still can, as long as the White man lives you will never be safe here."

But blaming Carlson and other right-wing media outlets for promoting this hatred is like blaming wet streets for rain. It was the Republican Party that ran a tweet on a huge video monitor at the 2016 Republican National Convention from VDARE.com, an anti-Semitic, racist organization listed as a hate group by the Southern Poverty Law Center. "Rep. Chris Collins has the crowd fired up against illegal immigration and for Donald Trump," read the tweet. And the people running the website were thrilled. "VDARE. Featured at the 2016 Republican Convention," they boast at the heading of their Twitter account.

————

It was the Republican Party that nominated and elected a racist in 2016, giving new meaning to the phrase "In America, anyone can grow up to be president." Yet while right-wing media has embraced racist conspiracies, the "mainstream media" in America has exhibited a strange aversion to labeling it what it is—racist. There's nothing new about this.

When David Duke ran for governor of Louisiana in 1991, the former Grand Wizard of the Ku Klux Klan was covered less as a candidate of racist anger than one of white economic frustration. "For thousands of Louisiana whites angry with hard times and high taxes, his is the ultimate 'no bull' campaign," *Newsweek* wrote.

This is the ship that launched a thousand profiles of "Trump voters in a diner," an entire genre of reportage dedicated to avoiding calling Trump a racist. For all the talk of Trump being a candidate of the "working class," he lost decisively among those who make $50,000 a year or less in both 2016 and 2020. But he won by large numbers those who were *white* and made $50,000 or less. In 2020, in fact, the only economic group Trump won were those who make $100,000 and over.

There is something almost amusing about this need to avoid the obvious, like dispatching America's best reporters to examine why men go to strip clubs. But gilding the brutal truth of racism in a coat of "economic anxiety" provides a dangerous cover for the legitimization of hate. The fact that Trump does have a very small minority of Black supporters no more disproves that he is a racist than a pack-a-day smoker who never gets lung cancer disproves the dangers of smoking.

Three Iowa State University sociologists conducted a detailed study of the thirty-one Iowa counties that flipped from Obama in 2008 to Trump in 2016, the most in the nation. Their study concluded, "Economic distress is not a significant factor in explaining the shift in Iowa voters from Democrat[ic] to Republican between 2008 and 2016." The sociologists—Ann Oberhauser, Daniel Krier, and Abdi Kusow—looked at household income, age, race, church attendance, and the "level of rurality" for each county, a data point that the Department of Agriculture calculates using the size of a county's population and its proximity to an urban area. "The election outcomes do not signify a revolt among working-class voters left behind by globalization." Instead, "the nativist narrative about taking back America and the anti-immigrant sentiment became stronger forces than economic issues." Consistent with other studies, the fear of immigrants escalated the highest in those areas that had the fewest number of immigrants. In counties where immigrants were actually living, voters were less likely to be moved by Trump's attacks on immigrants.

The belief is strong among those who embrace autocracy that democracy is destroying both their vision of the "real" America and their assumed standing in their own country. Theirs is a movement driven by racial fear. The United States will become a minority-majority country, and all the Stephen Millers in the world can't stop that. How fast is America changing? In 1980, Ronald Reagan won a sweeping landslide victory over Jimmy Carter, garnering 489 electoral votes with 56 percent of the white vote. In 2012, Mitt Romney lost to Barack Obama and received...59 percent of the white vote.

It is the failure to appeal to non-white voters in a rapidly changing country that is at the root of the transformation of the Republican Party into an autocratic movement. In an ever-increasing non-white America, the party faced two choices for survival—do what it took to appeal to more non-white voters or make it more difficult for non-white voters to participate. Tragically for democracy, the party took the second path.

The greatest danger can be a failure to recognize the greatest danger. If America slides from democracy to autocracy, it will be because those who support democracy cannot imagine an America without a democracy. These are people—those who are opposed to Trump and all he stands for—who believe in the politics of inevitability. They still see political differences occurring on a left-right, liberal-conservative axis that the autocrats have abandoned. It is naïve and foolish but predictable. They imagine that there is a *possibility* for the Republican Party to become a "normal" American political party once again.

It is a belief driven by an understandable inability of those who oppose Trump to accept that a huge percentage of Americans no longer believe they live in a democracy. It requires dangerously ignoring the fact that most Republicans do not believe Joe Biden was legally elected, which means they wake up every day in an occupied country.

The 2024 election will not be between two parties with competing views of how a democratic government should operate. It will be between one party that believes America is still a democracy and one that believes we have an illegal president in the White House. This has never happened before, and the ramifications of this are as unpredictable as they are profound. Millions of these Americans believe they must do whatever it takes to end this tyranny in America and that they have an *obligation* to do what is necessary.

The millions of Americans who believe democracy has abandoned them make no secret of insisting that they live in the "true" America. They show loyalty to their concept of their country by waving TRUMP and MAGA flags, while Trump himself assures them that they are special, even superior. "You have good genes, you know that, right?" he asked his supporters while campaigning in the northern Midwest in 2020. "You have good genes. A lot of it's about the genes, isn't it? Don't you believe? The racehorse theory you think was so different? You have good genes, Minnesota."

And the divisions between us aren't simply geographic. More than 6 million Californians voted for Trump in 2020, more than any other state. Drive through Upstate New York and Trump flags are everywhere. It is an identity, not a location.

This sense of living in a separate reality has been an essential element of right-wing media for some time. In her in-depth history of conservative media, *Messengers of the Right*, historian Nicole Hemmer traces the rise of a conservative media that defined itself as being the sole honest truth-teller among a legion of liberal-media liars. The origins are shockingly ironic. First published in the 1940s, the newsweekly known as *Human Events* was the Steve Jobs's garage of the alternative conservative media. What began as a few pages produced out of a Washington, D.C., apartment influenced the creation of the first major conservative book-publishing company, Regnery Publishing, the launching of William F. Buckley Jr.'s career, the founding of the John Birch Society, and the takeover of the Republican Party by Barry Goldwater conservatives.

When I was coming up in politics, *Human Events* was considered so kookily right-wing that it was known as "Inhuman Events." I always assumed that it must have been the creation of ultra right-wing crazies. While the two founders, Felix Morley and Frank Hannigan, were sympathetic to the America First movement of the 1930s—which had a broad anti-Semitic and fascist-sympathizing element—both were genuinely motivated by anti-war sentiments. Morley was a graduate and later president of Haverford College, a college outside Philadelphia founded by Quakers. When he was president of Haverford, Morley wrote a cover story for the *Saturday Evening Post* titled "For What Are We Fighting?" that was a rare argument against the war post–Pearl Harbor. In the 1930s, Hannigan wrote a critical examination of the global arms trade, a book titled *Merchants of Death*.

Today's divide between right-wing media and "mainstream media" was born in the conviction of Morley and Hannigan that American journalism had been corrupted by pro-war jingoism. As Hemmer writes:

> In the 1940s, the founders of Human Events were less concerned with the liberalism of the media than with the blackout of their nonconformist ideas. They believed mainstream American journalists were shutting out alternative points of view, that they were "coloring, slanting, selecting, and editing the

news" to tamp down any criticisms of the war. Morley argued that in trumpeting the official line doled out by government agencies, journalists had played a role in the "subtle regimentation of public opinion."

Morley and Hannigan were not alone in their concerns about the power of electronic media when post–World War II radio, then television, exploded in audience size. The Federal Communications Commission's 1949 "Fairness Doctrine" was a confusing attempt to require the media to present a balanced view of critical issues. In practice and execution, it was inevitably a mess, with people at every point on the ideological spectrum feeling their opinions were being suppressed by a powerful governmental hand. When the doctrine was allowed to die in 1987, any government effort to regulate political extremism on publicly licensed radio and television died with it.

Rush Limbaugh's weekday radio rant launched that same year. As historians Kevin Kruse and Julian Zelizer wrote in a 2019 *Washington Post* article titled "How Policy Decisions Spawned Today's Hyperpolarized Media," "Almost overnight, the media landscape was transformed. The driving force was talk radio. In 1960, there were only two all-talk radio stations in America; by 1995, there were 1,130. While television news on the old networks and the cable upstart CNN still adhered to the standard of objectivity, radio emerged as a wide-open landscape." Conservative listeners dominated the audience. "By 1995, conservatives accounted for roughly 70 percent of all talk radio listeners," Kruse and Zelizer wrote. "The end of the Fairness Doctrine had drastically changed the standards of news."

The concept of alienation from what we now call "mainstream media" that drove the founding of *Human Events* explains why only 30 percent of the new talk radio outlets were not conservative. The majority of citizens who did *not* identify themselves as hardcore conservatives were content with the news coverage and editorial approach of the dominant established media. As of 1986, Gallup found that 65 percent of Americans still felt a "great deal" or a "fair amount" of confidence in the press.

By 2000, trust in the media began to split sharply along partisan lines. Working in Republican politics, I saw it unfold. When I was working in the Bush campaign in 2000, the *New York Times* would post its next day's edition on the web every night at about midnight Eastern Time. At our campaign headquarters in Austin, about fifteen minutes after the *Times* went up, emails and phone calls would begin to come in from reporters covering the campaign for different media organizations, everyone following up on what the *Times* had published, the "newspaper of record" functioning as a de facto assignment editor for campaign coverage.

Today only 14 percent of Republicans say they have a fair

amount of trust in the media; the majority of Republicans say they have zero trust. Democrats' level of trust in the media has remained fairly constant since Gallup starting tracking and is now at 70 percent. Among self-declared independents, that trust has dropped to 27 percent.

Partisans' Trust in Mass Media, 1972-2022

% Great deal/Fair amount of trust and confidence in the mass media to report the news fully, accurately and fairly

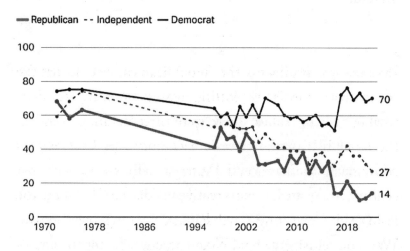

This complete breakdown of trust in the media by Republicans allows them to live in an alternative reality, one of their own making. In 2018, three Harvard professors—Yochai Benkler, Robert Faris, and Hal Roberts—made an exhaustive analysis of all aspects of information sources in the presidential campaign beginning in 2015. Their resulting book, *Network Propaganda*, is the most conclusive study of the impact on the American electorate of the current jumbled mix of political information voters receive—ranging from social media to traditional network news. The professors draw two basic conclusions: "First, having a segment of the population that is systematically disengaged from objective journalism and the ability to tell truth from partisan fiction is dangerous to any country. It creates fertile ground for propaganda. Second, it makes actual governance difficult."

———

Like many conspiracies, the Republican conviction that the "mainstream media" is plotting against them has an identifiable basis in reality. There were three defining events in the latter half of the twentieth century: the Civil Rights Movement, Vietnam, and Watergate. By the end of that century, three times conservative media had been on the losing side—rejecting Civil Rights, favoring the Vietnam War, and refusing to hold Nixon accountable for the abuses of power revealed during the Watergate investigation.

A generation of journalists was shaped by these events. In 1971, an Indiana University poll found that about 26 percent of journalists identified themselves as Republicans, 36 percent as Democrats, and 32 percent as independents. More than forty years later, those ratios had shifted dramatically. A 2013 survey found that only 7 percent of the nation's journalists considered themselves Republicans—and it's hard to imagine that number hasn't collapsed even more since Trump emerged as a Republican politician.

Self-identified Democratic journalists declined as well, but by a much smaller percentage, while the number who identified as independents soared. In part, these numbers reflect the societal trend of increased independent affiliation, but the facts are plain: Conservatives have increasingly been less represented in mainstream journalism than their counterparts.

It's a finding that tracks with another compelling statistic in the same survey. In 1971, 58 percent of journalists were college graduates. By 2013, that percentage had risen to 92 percent. The core of Republican support was and has long been non-college-educated whites. In 1980, when Reagan won a sweeping landslide, they comprised 65 percent of American voters. Today, they make up less than 40 percent—the fastest declining single demographic in the American electorate.

In his 1995 essay outlining the signposts of fascism, philosopher and linguist Umberto Eco pointed out the way in which authoritarians' loathing of learning is a sign they have moved from conservatism to fascism. "The Enlightenment, the Age of Reason, is seen as the beginning of modern depravity" to the fascist, and "thinking is a form of emasculation.... Distrust of the intellectual world has always been a symptom of Ur-Fascism."

When I started working in Republican campaigns in the 1980s, it was a given that the press favored Democrats. ANNOY THE MEDIA: RE-ELECT BUSH was a favorite bumper sticker in the 1992 campaigns. My standard line was that, for Republicans, the press "was always an away game after a long bus ride."

It wasn't that you couldn't overcome the home-team advantage the other side had, but it just made everything a little more difficult. George H. W. Bush was one of the youngest Navy pilots in World War II, flew fifty-eight missions and was shot down at age nineteen, then was rescued at sea after bailing out of his fighter bomber. He was labeled a "wimp." I worked for Mitt Romney in his 2012 campaign and saw him often portrayed as the cartoon of a heartless corporate raider, eager to inflict pain on the less fortunate. That wasn't who Mitt Romney was and I think it's fair to say that the public has had an opportunity to get a better sense of Mitt Romney as he became the only senator in U.S. history to vote to impeach a member of his own party, and joined a Black Lives Matter march in Washington.

But neither Bush nor Romney became haters of the press. Neither did George H. W. Bush's son, George W. Bush. When the press was swooning over John McCain at the height of his Straight Talk Express glory days before the 2000 New Hampshire primary, I observed up close how then-Governor Bush reacted. I can remember being on a bus with him after one of our less-than-raucous rallies and watching on the bus's television the glowing coverage of a McCain town hall meeting. Bush laughed. "They sure are having a lot more fun than we are. There's a lesson there," he said. "We have to do this better. I have to get better."

As much as Republicans complained about the media, going into the 2016 Republican primary the dirty little secret was that candidates desperately courted approval from the hated mainstream media. And they did so with success. A crank so unlikable that his neighbor finally had enough and beat him up, Rand Paul was on the cover of *Time*, a magazine that labeled him "The Most Interesting Man in Politics." I had friends who worked in the Paul campaign, and they spent a great deal of time courting reporters, as did Paul himself. So did Ted Cruz and his campaign. A uniquely despicable man who has such little self-respect that he begged Trump for his endorsement after Trump linked his father to the JFK assassination and insulted his wife's appearance, Cruz was profiled favorably in *The New Yorker*, which noted that he wore cowboy boots in front of a painting of Ronald Reagan.

It's difficult to find anyone in American politics more obsessed with his press coverage than Donald Trump. Before running for president, he had spent decades cultivating reporters, desperate for any attention he could get. Trump brilliantly understood that he could stand in front of a rally that felt more like a lynch mob than a political event and attack the press as "the enemy of the people," yet still be treated fairly by the media. As Harvard political science professors Steven Levitsky and Daniel Ziblatt write in *How Democracies Die*, "The tragic paradox of the electoral route to authoritarianism is that democracy's assassins use the very institutions of democracy—gradually, subtly, and even legally—to kill it."

For the traditional media—or "legacy media," or "mainstream media"—the greatest value has long been held to be objectivity. This attempt at neutrality has functioned with varying degrees of success in a system in which, historically, there was a basic assumption of mutual good faith. There were routine confrontations between a government trying to hide the truth and journalists trying to uncover the truth, but in the end, those confrontations almost invariably resulted in an affirmation of the value of a free press.

Politicians fought with the press constantly, but until Donald Trump, no figure was embraced by a major political party who attacked the press using the language of Joseph Stalin, who called the press the "enemy of the people." Even after Stalin's death, the Soviet Union's Nikita Khrushchev disavowed the phrase in 1956 in an address to the closed session of the Twentieth Congress of the Communist Party. "Stalin originated the concept 'enemy of the people,'" Khrushchev stated. "It made possible the use of the cruelest repression, against anyone who in any way disagreed with Stalin, against those who were only suspected of hostile intent, against those who had bad reputations."

It's a stunning irony: A leader of the Soviet Union—long hailed by Republicans as all that was evil—showed more honesty, self-awareness, and courage than have the leaders of the current Republican Party. In a world in which facts do not matter and there is no information bound by even the remotest guidelines of truth, the Republican Party's path down the dark road of autocracy will only accelerate. Today, Republican candidates and officeholders routinely block the media from their events, inviting only their handpicked and highly reliable propagandists to cover even the most routine functions. For them, the decision is only logical: Why should they allow the enemies of the people any opportunity to spread their dishonest narratives?

Until the Republican Party can summon at least a post-Stalin level of honesty, it will spin further and further away from what once was assumed to be the center of gravity in American life. As Donald Trump defended the results of his disastrous trade policy, he warned his followers: "What you're seeing and what you're reading is not what's happening." As George Orwell predicted in *1984*, "The party told you to reject the evidence of your eyes and ears. It was their final, most essential command."

Chapter 2

The Support of the Party

Sometimes party loyalty asks too much.

—President John F. Kennedy

It was the last stand. The move to stop Donald Trump from securing the 2016 Republican presidential nomination came down to a fight among members of the Platform Committee and the Rules Committee—two obscure elements of the Republican National Convention, which was held in Cleveland that year. Just over a year after Trump announced his candidacy, and after twelve debates, and elections in fifty states plus the District of Columbia and five U.S. territories, there was still a sense of disbelief among many in the party that a man who said publicly that he'd date "piece of ass" Ivanka if she were not his daughter would ultimately be the Republican nominee.

This Alamo in defense of decency was fought in the back rooms in Cleveland. The goal of the anti-Trump forces fighting in the Rules Committee was to "guarantee delegates the option to vote their conscience when picking the party's presidential nominee—rather than adhere to the results of primaries and caucuses," as *Politico* described it. The fight in the Platform Committee was to stop Trump from abandoning the basic principles that the party had espoused for decades.

I had worked in five presidential campaigns on the Republican side by that time, and I watched the anti-Trump forces with the certainty that they stood no better odds than those rag-tag Texian soldiers who attempted to hold an old adobe mission from the advance of Santa Anna's troops back in 1836. But at least they were fighting because they believed in something.

It's a sign of how desperate I was to find any sign of life in the Republican Party that I was actually cheering on the sidelines for the despicable Ted Cruz, who was a leader of this doomed-to-fail rebellion. This was the Ted Cruz about whom Al Franken had said, "Here's the thing you have to understand about Ted Cruz. I like Ted Cruz more than most of my other colleagues like Ted Cruz. And I hate Ted Cruz."

I'd had a similar experience with him. When I was working for Governor George Bush in the 2000 presidential campaign, I heard that a collegiate debating whiz named Ted Cruz was working for the campaign. I asked around about why he wasn't helping us with debate prep, and the answer was always, "Have you met him?" Once I did, I understood. But there was a brief moment at the 2016 convention in which I believed even this smarmiest of politicians was preferable to Trump. Unlike the other candidates whom Trump had defeated in the 2016 primary, Cruz was still refusing to endorse Trump—which, on any normal human scale of decency, made sense. And say what you will about Cruz being an intensely unlikable freak, he was also a genuine conservative who understood that the nuclear triad was not a hot threesome with models, an ignorance of Trump's that Hugh Hewitt exposed when he posed a primary-debate question to Trump. "Of the three legs of the triad, though, do you have a priority?" Hewitt asked Trump. "I think, I think, for me," stammered Trump, "nuclear is just the power, the devastation is very important to me."

Although the only alternative to stopping Trump at the convention had come down to Ted Cruz, watching that doomed effort made it possible for me and others to muster some semblance of hope that the Republican Party might actually stand up to Trump. Before the convention, once it had become clear that Trump *was* going to win the nomination, I approached a number of prominent Republicans from key states like Florida, North Carolina, and Pennsylvania, attempting to enlist them to run as independent candidates in their home states. It was reasonable to assume that if they drew just a few percentage points from Trump, he could not win those states and would be blocked from the presidency.

Their reactions uniformly went like this: "If we, the party establishment, put our thumbs on the scale, when Trump loses, it will not be because of his xenophobia, his racism, his anger. It will be our fault. We just have to let him lose and start over."

I would invariably respond, "But what if he wins?" And the answer always was, "He's not going to win." I didn't think he'd win either, so I probably wasn't very good at arguing the case.

But any last-stand efforts to stop Trump at the 2016 convention drew little support and Trump's dominance of the Republican Party was complete. Four years later, at the 2020 Republican Convention, there wasn't a platform fight—because for the first time in modern history, there was *no platform*. Instead, convention delegates approved just a few resolutions consisting of two main themes: proclamations of support for Trump and bashing the media critical of Donald Trump.

> *RESOLVED*, That the Republican Party has and will continue to enthusiastically support the President's America-first agenda;
>
> *RESOLVED*, That the Republican National Convention will adjourn without adopting a new platform until the 2024 Republican National Convention;
>
> *RESOLVED*, That the 2020 Republican National Convention calls on the media to engage in accurate and unbiased reporting, especially as it relates to the strong support of the RNC for President Trump and his Administration.

It's often said that Donald Trump has a cultlike following. But that's far too benign. The film *Star Wars* has a cultlike following. Taylor Swift has her cult of "Swifties." A political organization that has no platform other than loyalty to the leader is not a cult, it's an autocratic movement. As Hannah Arendt wrote in *The Origins of Totalitarianism*:

> Total loyalty is possible only when fidelity is emptied of all concrete content, from which changes of mind might naturally arise. The totalitarian movements, each in its own way, have done their utmost to get rid of the party programs which specified concrete content and which they inherited from earlier, non-totalitarian stages of development.

It seems like another time in another galaxy, but not that long ago, there actually *was* some ideological diversity within the Republican Party. In 1966, *Time* ran a cover story highlighting the winners of the 1966 midterm elections as a "Republican Resurgence," following the Goldwater massacre of 1964. *Time*'s editors selected six Republicans as being emblematic of this rebirth: California Governor Ronald Reagan, Michigan Governor George Romney, Illinois Senator Charles Percy, Oregon Senator Mark Hatfield, Massachusetts Senator Edward Brooke, and New York Governor Nelson Rockefeller. The six governors and senators had differences of opinion on almost all major issues.

Mark Hatfield, deeply influenced by his service in

World War II—which included his being one of the first Americans to visit Hiroshima following the dropping of the atomic bomb—never voted for a bill to authorize U.S. military engagement. He was one of only two Republican senators who voted against the 1991 Gulf War. With Senator George McGovern, Hatfield cosponsored 1971 legislation calling for a complete withdrawal from Vietnam.

Reagan, on the other hand, was consistently supportive of the Vietnam War and campaigned against the creation of Medicaid. Charles Percy voted for the Civil Rights Act of 1968 and, after reading *The Autobiography of Malcolm X*, said, "Every white person should read it." Today, in comparison, Florida Governor Ron DeSantis is running for president proudly touting that AP African American Studies violated his "Stop WOKE Act" and "lacked educational value."

In the 1990s and early 2000s, the Republican governors who were pro-choice governed states with a larger collective population than the Republican anti-abortion governors. Bill Weld of Massachusetts, Pennsylvania's Tom Ridge, Arnold Schwarzenegger in California, and New York's George Pataki all were proudly pro-choice. Today there are no Republican governors who support abortion rights, and many are actively working to criminalize abortions in their states. The Republican Party of three decades past was overwhelmingly a white-dominated party, but it allowed for at least some dissent and disagreement.

While it is difficult to attribute any deliberate or methodical plan to Donald Trump, whose mind operates like an old-fashioned pinball machine on tilt—bouncing from one inchoate impulse to another—his basic anti-democratic, Strongman instincts have crushed dissent in the Republican Party, empowering the underlying authoritarian impulses within the party. A once-center-right political party with core ideological principles is now marching toward the formation of an autocratic state.

———

It's possible that Donald Trump will not be the Republican nominee in 2024, but his success in molding the party to his image ensures that anyone who wins will continue down an authoritarian path. When Ron DeSantis ran for governor of Florida in 2018, he aired a commercial showing his toddler daughter building a border wall with toy blocks, followed by a shot of him holding his infant son and reading, "Then Mr. Trump said, 'You're fired,'" from a book, while the words PITBULL TRUMP DEFENDER were displayed on the screen. His wife also appeared in the ad, saying, "People say Ron is all Trump, but he is so much more."

As DeSantis campaigns for the Republican nomination, he is running as a cultural warrior, desperate to appeal to the Trump base. What's unfolding in the Republican Party is an inevitable step in the cycle of authoritarian movements. What once was deemed sufficiently pure is judged to be inadequate and in need of purging. DeSantis is running a bathroom and bedrooms campaign, his campaign slogan "Florida is where woke goes to die." I'm sure everyone wearing body paint at Fantasy Fest in Key West is happy to know Governor DeSantis is on the case. Trump dismisses DeSantis's obsession. "I don't like the term 'woke' because I hear, 'Woke, woke, woke,'" Trump said campaigning in Iowa. "It's just a term they use, half the people can't even define it, they don't know what it is."

"You've got elements of all the different branches of the Republican Party that see darkness now," David Gergen, a former advisor to Presidents Gerald Ford, Ronald Reagan, and Bill Clinton, told the *New York Times*. "Social conservatives have been at the forefront of that for a long time. But now the foreign policy and economic types feel like we face serious risk of decline." The Night of the Long Knives, the murder of Trotsky, the Red Guards, and the Khmer Rouge—each was the result of a radical movement further purifying its core membership and ideology, and something very similar is taking place among today's Republicans.

When Trump emerged in 2015, he was initially rejected by Republican voters. In a May 2015 CNN poll, Donald Trump polled at 3 percent among Republicans and Republican-leaning independent voters. While it's not unusual for a new and still-unknown candidate to start with a low number, Trump had almost a 100 percent name recognition among potential voters.

Republicans knew who he was; they just didn't like him. A May 2015 *Washington Post*–ABC News poll found that only 16 percent of Republicans viewed Trump favorably.

By early December 2015—and following his attack on John McCain's war record, his mocking of a disabled reporter, and calling for a Muslim ban—Trump had surged to his largest lead during the Republican primary, opening up a 35 percent to 16 percent lead over Ted Cruz. Jeb Bush, who led the field in early polling, was now at the same 3 percent level of support that Trump had in May.

The media coverage of Trump's rise evidenced an unwillingness to grasp Trump's appeal. "Donald Trump Leads Florida Polls, Despite Call for Muslim Travel Ban" was the headline in the *New Times Broward–Palm Beach*. "Trump Poll Surge Continues Despite Backlash Over Muslim Ban," trumpeted the December 10, 2015, broadcast of *Voice of America News*.

This was like reporting that Jim Beam sold a lot of bourbon even though it contained alcohol. Trump was rising with Republican voters *because* of his racism and religious bigotry. There was no backlash with the majority of Republican primary voters. The exact opposite was occurring. Trump's hate was creating a surge of appeal.

Donald Trump understood the true nature of the Republican Party better than those who were the party's leaders. "This suggestion is completely and totally inconsistent with

American values," Senate Majority Leader Mitch McConnell said as he denounced Trump's proposed Muslim ban. "I do not think a Muslim ban is in our country's interest," Speaker of the House Paul Ryan said. "I do not think it is reflective of our principles, not just as a party but as a country." But it was his call for a Muslim ban that helped Trump clinch the 2016 nomination.

McConnell and Ryan and the establishment donor class of the Republican Party would never admit publicly that the xenophobia and racism that appealed to Trump voters was far more motivating to Republican voters than the small government, low taxes, constitutionally conservative so-called "values" they insisted were the true core of the Republican Party. The absurdity of their deceit could not have been more glaringly obvious. Their commitment to their deeply held beliefs was so weak that they now supported a man who bragged he was "the king of debt," refused to release his tax returns to show he even paid taxes, and his Muslim ban was a religious test that was a clear violation of Article VI of the Constitution that "no religious Test shall ever be required as a Qualification to any Office or public Trust under the United States." They didn't care about anything but remaining in power. The Republican Party leadership was a collection of liars and frauds who thought they could use Trump while controlling him.

In their 2018 book *How Democracies Die*, Harvard University political scientists Steven Levitsky and Daniel Ziblatt describe the essence of the Republican Party's failure:

> An essential test for democracies is not whether [authoritarians] emerge but whether political leaders, and especially political parties, work to prevent them from gaining power in the first place—by keeping them off mainstream party tickets, refusing to endorse or align with them, and when necessary, making common cause with rivals in support of democratic candidates. Isolating popular extremists requires political courage. But when fear, opportunism, or miscalculation leads established parties to bring extremists into the mainstream, democracy is imperiled.

That is the test my former party failed. What happened within the Republican Party in 2016 was a repeat of the rise of National Socialism in 1920s and 1930s Germany. The aristocrats who were the power center in German politics realized they had lost touch with the working class of Germany. They saw an alliance with Adolf Hitler's party as the only way to stop the spreading appeal of Bolshevism. Even in 1952, former German Chancellor Franz von Papen—the man who ushered Hitler into power—attempted to justify his actions. "We found ourselves obliged to combat the doctrines of totalitarian Bolshevism," he wrote in *Memoirs of Franz von Papen*—making a plea for historical forgiveness based on the choices he and his fellow conservatives faced. "The fact that many of us saw in the anti-Communist attitude of the growing Nazi party the possibility of finding a new and useful ally may cause our errors to be viewed by historians in a slightly less critical light."

The American journalist William Shirer, who saw it all unfold while reporting from Berlin, described what occurred in his classic *The Rise and Fall of the Third Reich*: "Papen and Hitler met secretly on January 4, 1933, and worked out a deal. They agreed to form a government in which Hitler would be chancellor and Papen vice-chancellor. In return for being top man, Hitler agreed to appoint a cabinet in which the non-Nazi reactionaries behind Papen would be in the majority."

Shirer sums the pact up in a description that is hauntingly descriptive of the Republican Party's acceptance of Donald Trump: "By means of a shabby political deal with the old-school reactionaries he privately detested, the former tramp from Vienna, the derelict of the First World War, the violent revolutionary, became Chancellor of the great nation."

Like Adolf Hitler, Trump hated the establishment figures who supported him, and they despised him. Like von Papen, they thought they could control him. "I think we're much more likely to change him because if he is president, he's going to have to deal with sort of the right-of-center world, which is where most of us are," Mitch McConnell said in June 2016 when it was clear Trump would be the nominee.

Like Adolf Hitler, Trump stocked his first Cabinet with establishment figures meant to reassure the business community and the Republican establishment. Rex Tillerson resigned as CEO of ExxonMobil to become secretary of state. Steven Mnuchin left a career at Goldman Sachs and various hedge funds on Wall Street to head the Treasury Department. Retired Marine General James Mattis, former head of the United States Central Command, became secretary of defense. Billionaire business executive Wilbur Ross, named by Bloomberg Markets as one of the fifty most influential people in global finance, took over the Commerce Department. Elaine Chao, Mitch McConnell's wife and a former labor secretary under President George W. Bush, was named transportation secretary. Except for a couple of oddball picks like Linda McMahon, former chief executive of World Wrestling Entertainment, at the Small Business Administration and Betsy DeVos, the wife of an Amway heir and former chair of the Michigan Republican Party, the first Trump Cabinet was one that any Republican president might have selected.

For a brief moment, this allowed so many Republican Party leaders who knew that Trump was a danger to the country—who knew they supported him only to boost their own power—to believe that Trump was a "normal"

Republican president, albeit one who possessed a few quirks. "He is not a perfect man," former Texas Governor Rick Perry said in May 2016. "But what I do believe is that he loves this country, and he will surround himself with capable, experienced people, and he will listen to them." This notion was reinforced by an almost comic refrain among journalists and pundits that once Trump was elected, people were eager to conclude that Trump had grown into the office. "He became President of the United States in that moment, period," declared CNN commentator Van Jones after Trump addressed a Joint Session of Congress. For his first year in office, this phrase was frequently repeated by pundits whenever Trump acted like a "normal" president until finally it became too absurd for even Fox News to pretend.

In the same way a deviant child loves to pull the wings off a butterfly, Trump reveled in mocking those who were eager to declare that he was suddenly acting like a president. "Do you know how easy it is to be presidential? But you'd all be out of here right now. You'd be so bored," Trump told a rally for U.S. Congressional candidate Rick Saccone of Pennsylvania in March 2018. Saccone lost his race a few days later.

Trump's initial Cabinet of mostly establishment figures quickly devolved into chaos, as did his entire White House operation. "Trump Cabinet Turnover Sets Record Going Back 100 Years," NPR reported. "In just fourteen months on the job, Trump has had more Cabinet turnover than sixteen of his predecessors had in their first two years."

In *The Origins of Totalitarianism*, historian Hannah Arendt describes the defining element essential to autocratic movements. "Compared with all other parties and movements, their most conspicuous external characteristic is their demand for total, unrestricted, unconditional, and unalterable loyalty of the individual member." Five months into his presidency, Trump summoned his Cabinet members for a bizarre public fealty test that looked more like North Korea than America as each secretary tried to outdo the other by slathering Trump with obsequious praise. Each of his appointees seated around the huge table spoke in turn, competing in this self-humiliation derby as the new president demanded. As the *Washington Post* reported, White House Chief of Staff Reince Priebus led off the groveling by thanking Trump "for the opportunity and blessing that you've given us to serve your agenda and the American people."

"It's an honor to be able to serve you," said Attorney General Jeff Sessions. "I am privileged to be here," said Labor Secretary Alexander Acosta. "What an incredible honor it is to lead the Department of Health and Human Services at this pivotal time under your leadership," Tom Price intoned, all but bowing. "I can't thank you enough for the privileges you've given me and the leadership that you've shown."

Trump's style of governing was straight from the

authoritarian playbook. As Ruth Ben-Ghiat writes in *Strongmen: Mussolini to the Present*, "In the strongman tradition, Trump has used divide-and-rule and bullying tactics to weed out government officials who won't conspire in his corruption and subversion of the rule of law."

Trump destroyed any pretense that the Republican Party was an organization dedicated to serving millions of members, some of them almost certainly holding differing opinions. In the classic autocratic style, the party became a tool to enforce Trump's power and enrich him and his inner circle.

Trump ran for office using his supposed wealth as a credential. There had been wealthy presidents before, but none had been elected arguing that *because* he was rich, he was qualified for office. "I have a total net worth of $8.73 billion," Trump declared when he entered the presidential race in the summer of 2015. "I'm not doing that to brag. I'm doing that to show that's the kind of thinking our country needs." His refrain that "I'm the most successful person ever to run for the presidency, by far" was Trump's essential qualification. "Nobody's ever been more successful than me. I'm the most successful person ever to run."

Trump used his manufactured image of being vastly wealthy to prove to his voters that he was above corruption. One of the foundational lies of the Trump campaign was that he was his own campaign's sole donor.

"You know a lot of times you see these really dumb deals,"

Trump told an Iowa audience before the 2016 Republican caucus. "And you'll say that's dumb. It doesn't make sense. But then when you think, it does make sense because these politicians are representing interests, whether it's a country or a company, where doing the stupid deals actually makes sense only for that politician and for that company or country." Trump was different, he claimed, because "I'm self-funding my own campaign. It's my money."

The obviousness of this lie should have been apparent to anyone who visited the Trump campaign website and saw the "Donate" button. "From the start of his campaign in April through October last year, individual contributions made up about 67 percent of the total money raised for his campaign," the Poynter Institute's *PolitiFact* wrote in an article called "Is Donald Trump Self-Funding His Campaign? Sort of." The assertion that Donald Trump was financing his own campaign was every bit as true as Vladimir Putin's claim that Russia invaded Ukraine to rid that country of Nazis. But truth means nothing to autocrats, and as Trump lied his way to the nomination, the embrace of his lies by the Republican Party was just another way he welcomed the entire party apparatus into the large criminal enterprise that was his campaign and, then, his presidency.

Trump's base of supporters didn't care if he used his office to enrich himself and his family because if being rich was a qualification for office, getting richer only proved you were *more* qualified. Trump is part of a wave of modern autocrats that Moisés Naim calls the "3P Autocrats" in his 2022 book *The Revenge of Power*—people for whom "populism, polarization, and post-truth are strategies." This newer breed of autocrats doesn't loot the wealth of the state brazenly, like Saddam Hussein or Vladimir Putin—men who "dip into their nation's coffers unrestrained by laws or institutions." "The 3P Autocrats," Naim writes, "need to be more careful about the ways they get rich, make others rich, and use money to fortify their regime. They still do all of that but more stealthily and while being more mindful of the need to look like democrats, honest government officials, and corruption-busters."

Together with Trump, Naim includes "Venezuela's Hugo Chávez, Hungary's Viktor Orbán, the Philippines' Rodrigo Duterte, India's Narendra Modi, Brazil's Jair Bolsonaro, Turkey's Recep Tayyip Erdoğan, and El Salvador's Nayib Bukele." All these leaders blurred the lines between politicians and celebrities. By establishing himself to be judged not as a regular politician, Trump could reject any of the normal standards for judging a politician. If a celebrity is wealthy, it's a sign of his success, Trump implicitly announced. Fans don't expect their favorite celebrities to live normal lives.

"When traditional politicians break an important norm, their supporters turn on them, and their political standing suffers," Naim writes. "But when celebrity leaders break an important norm, their fans don't turn on the leaders; they turn on the norm. In fact, they rally to the leaders, who's standing often improves, at least in the fans' eyes."

————————

For autocratic movements to succeed, all power must be centralized under a single authority. For all true American conservatives, however, that reality violates every Federalist-driven gene in their political bodies—something like a Southern Republican attacking welfare while on welfare. Well, actually, they do that regularly since every Republican politician in Alabama, Mississippi, Georgia, South Carolina, Arkansas, and Florida are well aware that their states get a huge hunk of their state budget from the federal government.

In the classic collection of essays *What Is Conservatism?*, published in 1964, longtime *National Review* editor Frank Meyer described the skepticism of the centralized power of the state as the unifying principle of conservatism:

> While there is great divergence among conservatives as to the degree to which the state must be limited, they all share, in contrast to contemporary Liberals, a distaste for the use of the power of the state to enforce ideological patterns upon human beings. However much they may differ on the modes by which, and the extent to which, the power of the state should be limited, they are in full agreement that it is but

one institution among many and that when its role is aggrandized in the fashion of the twentieth century it becomes dangerous beyond measure.

Yet these days, Republicans have a relationship with federalism that is exactly like their relationship with activist judges. They are for federalism when it gives power to the states to oppose a piece of legislation they don't like. They are against federalism when it conflicts with their agenda. Anti-abortion activists spent decades, for example, calling for the repeal of *Roe v. Wade* so that states could decide their own policies. "Today's decision by the Supreme Court is a long overdue constitutional correction allowing for elected officials in the states to decide issues of life," South Carolina Republican Senator Lindsey Graham tweeted on June 24, 2022. Two months later, he introduced legislation for a federal bill banning abortion in all states after fifteen weeks of gestation.

Once a political party in a democratic system abandons any moral or ideological rationale for its existence, it is on the road to autocracy. After the Republican Party accepted a platform that was nothing more than a fealty pledge to Donald Trump, it surrendered any pretense of being anything other than an autocratic movement. If Trump is not ultimately the party's nominee in 2024, its loyalty will pass to the next leader. Ruth Ben-Ghiat describes the process in *Strongmen: Mussolini to the Present*:

Once the ruler is in power, elites strike an "authoritarian bargain" that promises them power and security in return for loyalty to the ruler and toleration of his suspension of rights. Some are true believers, and others fear the consequences of subtracting their support, but those who sign on tend to stick with the leader through gross mismanagement, impeachment, or international humiliation.

That is a perfect description of how Republican elites have been used by Donald Trump. They are part of a ritual in which everyone knows her or his role. All of them are allowed to pretend they can disagree with their Strongman—as Mitch McConnell did after the January 6, 2021, insurrection. "There is no question, none, that President Trump is practically and morally responsible for provoking the events of that day," McConnell intoned on the floor of the Senate. "The people who stormed this building believed they were acting on the wishes and instructions of their president." But McConnell spoke only after voting *not* to convict Trump for his role in inciting the riot.

Just as Vladimir Putin allowed limited dissent for most of his two-decade rule in Russia prior to his February 2022 invasion of Ukraine, Republican elected officials and party officials know some expression of disagreement is beneficial to the illusion that the party is a normally functioning one.

In his role as chairman of the Republican Senatorial Committee in 2022, Senator Rick Scott published "An Eleven Point Plan to Rescue America: What Americans Must Do to Save This Country." In addition to the curious detail that the eleven-point plan actually had *twelve* points, the most notable of them was a pledge to require a vote on all federal programs every five years. "All federal legislation sunsets in five years," Scott maintained. "If a law is worth keeping, Congress can pass it again."

Most of the party acted as if Rick Scott were some oddball stranger who'd wandered off the street into the Republican Senatorial Committee and wasn't, in fact, the chairman of that same committee, elected by the Republican Senate caucus. Mitch McConnell joined with then–Minority Leader Kevin McCarthy to dismiss Scott and his plan. "I think we're in a more authoritative position to state what the position of the party is than any single senator," McConnell said in an interview shortly after Scott released his plan. "It's just a bad idea." Then he taunted his fellow senator with the prospect of having to defend the plan. "I think it will be a challenge for him to deal with this in his own re-election in Florida, a state with more elderly people than any other state in America."

Trump piled on. "Under no circumstances should Republicans vote to cut a single penny from Medicare or Social Security," he claimed. Yet all of this was basic political theater with no consequence whatsoever. It allowed Mitch McConnell and Kevin McCarthy to present an illusionary image that they were powerful and in control. "Rick Scott's agenda is seen as challenge to McConnell by some in the GOP," led an NBC News story at the time.

It's all meaningless as everyone involved knows. No one has crossed the Red Line that the party enforces—unwavering support for Donald Trump. Mitch McConnell—who so bravely called out Rick Scott—is afraid to even utter Donald Trump's name. "Let me just say again, there is simply no room in the Republican Party for antisemitism or white supremacy," McConnell told reporters after Trump met with Holocaust denier and professional anti-Semite Nick Fuentes. "That would apply to all of the leaders in the party who will be seeking offices," McConnell added, carefully refusing to name Donald Trump as if there were suddenly *dozens* of Republicans eager to meet with Holocaust deniers.

Neither would Kevin McCarthy mention Donald Trump by name. "I don't think anybody should have a meeting with Nick Fuentes, and his views are nowhere within the Republican Party or within this country itself," he told reporters— as if he had heard that someone, somewhere, might have met with the white supremacist but McCarthy had no idea who it was.

At a moment when Donald Trump was simply a retired federal employee living in Florida—someone with no official position, a disgraced, twice-impeached ex-president who incited a mob that attempted to kill McConnell's and McCarthy's colleagues—the two highest elected officials in the Republican Party were afraid to even speak the man's name. This is how autocracies work. Fear is the organizing emotion of authoritarianism, just as hope is the defining element of democracy.

———

When the Republican Party operated as a traditional American party, it defined itself as the party of hope—one that believed in the "politics of inevitability" that Timothy Snyder describes. It was hope that drove the invention of America. "The establishment of our new Government seemed to be the last great experiment, for promoting human happiness, by reasonable compact, in civil Society," George Washington wrote nine months into his first term in a letter to Catharine Macaulay, one of the first female historians and a prominent English supporter of the American revolution. When Abraham Lincoln wrote that America was "the last best hope of earth," it was not a radical statement but a reminder of a shared conviction. Lincoln was appealing to a fundamental belief that united Americans at a time when other forces were tearing apart the social fabric that made America a country.

All political parties use fear of an opponent to unify

supporters, and they always have. When Democrats attack Republicans by saying Medicare cuts will effectively roll old ladies in wheelchairs off cliffs, that's fear. When Nixon ran on his infamous law-and-order platform in 1968, it was very much a strategy based on fear. What is different about the current Republican Party is that fear is its organizing principle, both internally and externally. The party drives support through fear and enforces discipline on the elected officials through fear.

January 6, 2021, was the defining moment of today's Republican Party. Fear drove the mob to the Capitol—and the mob was called to action by a fearful leader. They were afraid of the choice 81 million Americans had made about who would be their next president, and they were fearful that their coalition consisted of 85 percent white voters was not big enough to win in 2020 America. They were terrified of what an inclusive, multicultural America could do to their status and superiority.

A panicked Senator Josh Hawley ran through the Capitol to escape the mob he had earlier encouraged with his prep school version of a raised fist. Mike Pence was worried that his Secret Service detail would drive away from the Capitol complex so he couldn't complete his constitutional duty. "I'm not getting in the car, Tim," Pence told his lead agent. "I trust you, Tim, but you're not driving the car. If I get in that vehicle, you guys are taking off. I'm not getting in the car."

On January 5, Mitch McConnell went to bed as majority leader of the U.S. Senate. A day later, he was a minority leader running for his life in his own office. But he still refused to convict Trump. Why? Fear. Can there be any greater example of cowardice than refusing to stand up to the man who sent a violent mob into your place of work intent on killing you and your coworkers?

Sixty-five percent of House Republicans voted to challenge the certification of the election. Those who led the rebellion were subsequently rewarded by the party. Representative Marjorie Taylor Greene is now the second most powerful member of Congress. Those who led the opposition have all been punished. There is no room for Liz Cheney in today's Republican Party.

A *Cheney*.

A few people in the party continued to denounce the violence of January 6, but officially, the party chose to censure both Liz Cheney and Adam Kinzinger. The wording of the censure itself is shockingly honest:

> WHEREAS, the primary mission of the Republican Party is to elect Republicans who support the United States Constitution and share our values....
>
> WHEREAS, Representatives Cheney and Kinzinger are participating in a Democrat-led persecution of ordinary citizens engaged in legitimate political

discourse, and they are both utilizing their past professed political affiliation to mask Democrat abuse of prosecutorial power for partisan purposes, therefore, be it

RESOLVED, that the Republican National Committee hereby formally censures Representatives Liz Cheney of Wyoming and Adam Kinzinger of Illinois and shall immediately cease any and all support of them as members of the Republican Party for their behavior which has been destructive to the institution of the U.S. House of Representatives, the Republican Party and our republic, and is inconsistent with the position of the Conference.

There it is. The Republican Party doesn't aim to improve the lives of Americans; it exists to elect Republicans who share...what values? Not the rule of law, not respect for others, not honoring a democratic system in which one side must be willing to lose, and certainly not a democracy that benefits all Americans. The only value in today's Republican Party is loyalty to the party—which is loyalty to the leader.

As is always the case when an authoritarian movement emerges from a democracy, the justification for abandoning democracy was the danger that democracy itself presented. The Cheney and Kinzinger censure motion led with a litany of the terrible fate awaiting America and Americans if the Democrats were allowed to continue to govern:

> WHEREAS, The Biden Administration and Democrats in Congress have embarked on a systematic effort to replace liberty with socialism; eliminate border security in favor of lawless, open borders; create record inflation designed to steal the American dream from our children and grandchildren; neuter our national defense and a peace through strength foreign policy; replace President Trump's "Operation Warp Speed" with incompetence and illegal mandates; and destroy America's economy with the Green New Deal.

The party line was clear: Refusal to investigate the most dangerous attack on the American Capitol since the War of 1812 is necessary to defeat a *greater* danger. The *real* threat to America is the newly elected president who received more votes than any American politician in history.

The official censure was a clear message that the Republican Party supported those who attacked the Capitol, calling it "legitimate political discourse." They would deny this was their intent, but for those haters who were drawn to violence, there could be no doubt that one party would support prosecuting them and another party would condone their violent actions. Both Donald Trump and Florida Governor Ron DeSantis have pledged to consider pardons for the insurrectionists if elected president. Once opposing terrorism was a threshold requirement in the Republican Party. Now it is supporting domestic terrorism.

At every point when the Republican Party faced a choice between functioning as a normal American political party and an autocratic movement, it rejected the norm and moved closer to autocracy. When Trump won in 2016, there was a need among many of my Republican friends to assert that Trump had somehow "hijacked" the party—like a terrorist taking over the cockpit of an airliner. It was a reassuring fantasy to assume that, at some point, order would be restored and the plane would safely continue to its destination.

When faced with even the most fundamental of choices—choosing between the domestic terrorists who attempted to kill their own party members and the brave law enforcement officers defending them—the Republican Party chose to defend and elevate the terrorists. This was a deliberate, calculated decision driven by the need to defend Donald Trump, not America.

The initial reaction from Republicans who were threatened by the mob was one of horror. Almost every Republican who was at the Capitol on January 6, 2021, immediately denounced the mob. Listen to this chorus from elected Republican officials in the first days following the insurrection:

Senator Mitch McConnell: "The mob was fed lies. They were provoked by the president and other powerful people.... They tried to disrupt our democracy, they failed."

Congressman Kevin McCarthy: "The violence, destruction, and chaos we saw earlier was unacceptable, undemocratic, and un-American. It was the saddest day I've ever had serving as a member of this institution.... We saw the worst of America this afternoon. The president bears responsibility for Wednesday's attack on Congress by mob rioters."

Vice President Mike Pence: "Today was a dark day in the history of the United States Capitol. We condemn the violence that took place here in the strongest possible terms. To those who wreaked havoc today, you did not win."

Congresswoman Elise Stefanik: "This has been a truly tragic day for America. And we all join together in fully condemning the dangerous violence and destruction that occurred today in our Nation's Capitol. Americans will always have the freedom of speech and the Constitutional right to protest, but violence in any form is absolutely unacceptable, it is anti-American, and must be prosecuted to the fullest extent of the law."

Senator Lindsey Graham: "When it comes to accountability, the president needs to understand that his actions were the problem, not the solution."

Senator Marsha Blackburn: "These actions at the U.S. Capitol by protestors are truly despicable and unacceptable. While I am safe and sheltering in place, these protests are prohibiting us from doing our constitutional duty. I condemn them in the strongest possible terms."

Senator Rick Scott: "No one has a right to commit violence. What happened today at the Capitol is disgraceful and un-American. It is not what our country stands for."

But quickly, the part of them that responded as Americans and decent citizens was crushed by the demands of the party that it was time to fall in line. Their brief encounter with what it was like to be a patriot who put country over party ended, and they transformed back from Americans into Party Apparatchiks.

Two weeks after the insurrection, Kevin McCarthy was once again the aging fraternity rush chairman who would do anything to be accepted by the Big Man on Campus fraternity president. "I don't believe he provoked it, if you listen to what he said at the rally," McCarthy argued as he now defended Trump.

And before January was out, McConnell affirmed that he would "absolutely" vote for Trump if he were the GOP nominee in 2024.

"Can we move forward without President Trump? The answer is no," Graham told Fox News host Sean Hannity. "I've determined we can't grow without him."

"We're ashamed of nothing," said Representative Matt Gaetz (R-FL) during an appearance with Representative Marjorie Taylor Greene (R-GA) on a podcast hosted by former Trump strategist Steve Bannon—who was indicted for defying a subpoena from the House committee investigating the insurrection. "We're proud of the work that we did on January 6 to make legitimate arguments about election integrity."

Nearly two years after the insurrection, Texas Senator Ted Cruz made the blandest of statements at a Senate Rules Committee oversight hearing on January 6 security failures. Cruz acknowledged the "solemn anniversary" of what he called a "violent terrorist attack on the Capitol where we saw the men and women of law enforcement...risk their lives to defend the men and women who serve in this Capitol."

But Cruz was immediately attacked by Tucker Carlson on Carlson's former Fox News show. "Of all the things that January 6 was," Carlson pontificated, "it was definitely not a violent terrorist attack." Hearing Carlson's rebuke, Cruz immediately asked to appear on his show to grovel. "It was a mistake to say that yesterday. The reason I used that word is that's the word I've always used for people that attack cops," he insisted.

Carlson was unsatisfied. He reveled in forcing Cruz to humiliate himself even more. "You called this a terror attack when by no definition was it a terror attack. That's a lie. You told that lie on purpose, and I'm wondering why you did. I do not believe that you used that accidentally. I just don't."

Cruz bowed even lower and begged for forgiveness. "As a result of my sloppy phrasing, it's caused a lot of people to misunderstand what I meant. What I was referring to was the limited number of people who engaged in violent attacks against police officers." Then he pivoted to attacking those who had consistently stood with the Capitol police. "But in this context, I get why people are angry. Because we've had a year of the corrupt corporate media and Democrats have so politicized it." Cruz finished by utterly aligning himself with the terrorists and their goals. "While thousands of people were standing up to defend this country on January 6," he claimed, "I was standing on the Senate floor, objecting to the election results."

The Republican transition from the "law and order party" to an organization explicitly condoning violent attacks on democracy became complete when Donald Trump began to hold rallies for his 2024 presidential campaign. In Trump world, the domestic terrorists of January 6 are heroes. The woman who broke through police lines and refused police orders to stop and was shot while attempting to climb through a barricaded door is a martyr. The National Anthem is converted to an insurrectionist rallying cry sung by prison inmates—all of them insurrectionists—who tried to steal democracy. The recording, titled "Justice for All," is the "J6 Prison Choir's" version of "The Star-Spangled Banner," with Trump reciting the Pledge of Allegiance. The Republican Party is not quietly attempting to appeal to the radicals who attempted to overthrow our government; the party is making a direct appeal for their support. Trump apocalyptically describes the next presidential election—which should be a celebration of democracy—as "the final battle."

Only a handful of Republican leaders say they will not support the man glorifying the end of American democracy if he is their party's nominee in 2024. The message could not be clearer. Those seeking to end democracy by violence are welcome in the Republican Party. During the 2020 campaign, the Lincoln Project—a collection of former Republican political consultants that I joined—posed a stark choice: America or Trump. That continues to be true, but the Republican Party's continuing embrace of authoritarianism makes the 2024 election an even more chilling choice: America or the Republican Party?

Chapter 3

The Financers

There are only two important things in politics. The
first is money, and I can't remember the second.

—*Mark Hanna (1837–1904),*
U.S. Senator, political boss

Money's influence moves American politics left and right, and it has since before the founding of the republic. For most of our country's history, this shift took place within the established norms of American democracy. There's always been far too much money in American politics. No other Western democracy allows vast sums of money to pollute its electoral system. Repeated efforts to change our system to limit the impact of money have largely failed. But until recently, spending in support of candidates and parties was intended to move our politics in an ideological direction. That's changed. Today staggering sums of money are being spent not to change the policies of our democracy but to end democracy.

Like many of the changes in our politics, most of it is happening in the open and is perfectly legal. Yet the increased financial power of anti-democratic actors has been largely overlooked in the chaos that defines the way in which we fund campaigns.

When you examine American political campaigns, you can't help but talk about money. "Former President Donald

Trump raised more than $4 million in the twenty-four hours after news of his indictment in Manhattan became public, according to figures released by his campaign Friday," NBC reported in March 2023. When a former president of the United States was indicted for the first time in history—and as Republicans attacked the very concept of the rule of law—the amount of money Trump raised and the speed with which he did so was considered an important part of the story.

And it's hard to argue it's not. Raising $4 million in twenty-four hours was a de facto instant poll demonstrating precisely how Trump's fundraising base felt about his "political persecution." "One of the major reasons Hillary Clinton had enjoyed front-runner status leading up to the 2008 Democratic primary contests was the belief that she would break all fundraising records," Lori Cox Han wrote in *In It to Win: Electing Madam President.* When Senator Barack Obama raised $36 million in comparison to Clinton's $13.5 million in January 2008, the Clinton campaign was widely portrayed as collapsing.

In that particular case, the money poll proved accurate, and it's a common assumption that money determines campaigns. A 2011 CNN/*USA Today*/Gallup poll asked American adults whether they agreed with the statement "Elections are generally for sale to the candidate who can raise the most money," 67 percent of the respondents agreed that, yes, political races *are* for sale.

In over 90 percent of the campaigns for the House of Representatives, the candidate with the most money wins. And overall, around 95 percent of incumbents win reelection. That was true in 1968 and was still true in 2022. Incumbents raise more money because they are incumbents, but they also win because they are incumbents.

There are a few instances where incumbents do lose in primaries despite outspending their opponents. In 2014, a Virginia college professor named David Brat spent just over $200,000 to defeat House Majority Leader Eric Cantor, who had raised $5.4 million as the incumbent. The brilliant UCLA political scientist Lynn Vavreck analyzed the impact for the *New York Times*. "Information collected by the Federal Election Commission over the last thirty years shows that 60 percent of congressional challengers since 1992 have spent less than $200,000 on their campaigns, accounting for inflation. Only 0.5 percent of them won. By comparison, fewer than 1 percent of incumbents spent so little money, and all of them won."

There exists a self-congratulatory quality to American democracy that shields public discussion from many difficult questions. Whenever the future of Russia is debated, the role that oligarchs will continue to play is invariably front and center in the discussion. The assumption is that the vastly wealthy group who surround Putin, known as the *Siloviki*, is a power center that plays a more important role in Russia than its citizens—who are rather euphemistically called *voters*. Although there are far more billionaires in America both in real terms—735 in the U.S. compared with 83 in Russia as of 2022—and three times more of them per capita, there is clearly a reluctance to acknowledge their power in the American political system. This is a combination of the reality that in the United States, our voters actually do matter, combined with a national need to believe that voters are *all* that matters.

When you compare the political influence of the vastly wealthy in Russia and the United States, you can make a good case that the *Siloviki* of America have more political power than their counterparts in Russia. As the recent Russian invasion of Ukraine proves, that nation is a dictatorship in which one man makes all the critical decisions and many smaller ones as well. When Vladimir Putin decided to invade a neighboring country, dooming hundreds of thousands of Russians and Ukrainians in a war of genocide, it was his decision alone. Western Russian observers speculated that Russian oligarchs might be able to press Putin to end the war. But it never happened. These men—and they are all men—who possess enormous money, influence, and power nonetheless wake up and fall asleep terrified of a single short former KGB agent who drove a St. Petersburg taxi in the 1990s. They know for a fact that a jail cell, an open window, or a slow death by poison is the fate of those who dare not obey the Russian czar.

In the American political system, on the other hand, it's the *politician* who wakes up and goes to bed fearing the very wealthy. For all the never-ending talk of campaign finance reform, the billionaire class has designed perfectly legal methods to exert tremendous influence over the democratic process. In theory, this is a power that is ideologically neutral, available to liberal billionaires like George Soros and libertarian conservatives like the Koch brothers. The same is also theoretically true of the First Amendment. Notionally, a powerful far-left television network—one operating with the same disregard for ethical journalism that epitomizes Fox News—could emerge and successfully compete with Fox News. But it has never happened and there is no reason to believe it will. So it is with campaign finance. The wealthy on the right have proven to be more effective exerting their influence than those on the center-left.

For most of the years that I worked in campaigns, the popular belief that politicians sell their votes never struck me as accurate. The assumption that a campaign contribution is a quid pro quo bribe, particularly in federal races that limit individual contributions to $2,700, does a disservice both to the criminality of actual bribes and the seriousness of the problem of money in our campaign culture. As UCLA law professor Richard Hasen, who has written extensively on election law, states in his 2016 book *Plutocrats United*, "The new *Citizens United* era is not full of corrupt politicians taking bribes or of elections going to the highest bidder. To claim it so puts the public's spotlight in the wrong place, looking for elected officials to use large amounts of money for private gain."

The corruption of money in the American political system is not so much the corruption of individual politicians but the corruption of the entire electoral process. It's not individual politicians who are compromised by our uniquely dysfunctional campaign finance reality but democracy itself. It's the voters who are corrupted unwillingly and unknowingly by being denied any option of participating in elections that are not affected by vast sums of money.

There are few who defend the current state of money in politics in America. But the consistency and duration of the problem have lent it a background noise quality, a bit like everyday banter about bad weather. Announcing that "there's too much money in politics" is like asking "hot enough for you?" in the midst of an Arizona summer. Even before there was the United States of America, money in politics was a problem.

In April 1699, the Virginia General Assembly passed a law prohibiting a candidate "or any persons on their behalf" from giving voters "money, meat, drink, entertainment, or provision or... any present, gift, reward, or entertainment, etc. in order to be elected." Two centuries later, U.S. President Theodore Roosevelt devoted whole sections of his 1904 and 1905 State of the Union speeches to calls for campaign-finance reform. "There is no enemy of free government more dangerous and none so insidious as the corruption of the electorate," he told Congress in 1904. A year later, he called for the banning of contributions by corporations and their directors, reforms that have never been universally enacted in American elections: "All contributions by corporations to any political committee or for any political purpose should be forbidden by law," Roosevelt contended.

What our long saga of attempted campaign reform reveals is the inherent futility of depending on American politicians to enact and enforce laws that are aimed at limiting their actions. Congress has a long history of doing the exact opposite, exempting itself from the laws it passes to govern the rest of us. Working in campaigns for over thirty years, I've seen the collapse of the effectiveness of campaign finance laws. I'm one of the few who have worked at a high level in presidential campaigns in both the old system of federal funding and following its collapse—and the magnitude of the difference between the two is enormous. Under the federal funding system, which began in 1976, each candidate who accepted a major-party nomination received the same amount of money in exchange for not raising or spending additional funds. This is why campaigns moved their nominating conventions back later and later in the election season. The same amount of money was available, and it made sense to compress the time in which it could be utilized in order to maximize impact. In the 2000 Bush campaign, we held the Republican convention in July, but moved it to late August in 2004, as close to the mandatory sixty-day deadline before the election as we could manage.

In 2008, Barack Obama—like every candidate in the two major parties running for the nomination that year—agreed to accept federal funding and abide by the limits. But once he realized how much money he could raise online, he reversed himself, becoming the first presidential nominee from a major party since the federal-funding law began in 1976 to walk away from the voluntary system. He raised and spent over $300 million in the general election, while John McCain stayed in the system and spent only the $84 million allocated under federal-funding rules. This effectively killed the public financing of presidential elections.

In 2012, both Mitt Romney and Barack Obama rejected federal funding, and each raised and spent over a billion dollars. I worked inside both the 2000 and the 2004 Bush campaigns, which accepted federal funds with spending limits, and the Romney campaign, which joined Obama in rejecting funding. The differences were stark. In the Romney campaign, we spent about 40 percent of our total post-convention campaign time raising money. There is nothing good about this. That's 40 percent less time meeting voters, talking to the media, and making a case to voters about who should be the next president.

The 2012 presidential campaign was the first since the Nixon-McGovern race in 1972 in which both candidates were not constrained by a federal funding system. The $2.5 billion spent by the combined campaigns was a sickening amount of money, even in a political system with a powerful addiction to money. But in one important aspect, the 2012 campaign operated within a norm that has existed throughout the modern era in American politics. Although the amount spent on behalf of the Obama and the Romney campaigns broke all records, most of that money was raised and spent by the campaigns themselves. Outside groups—what have come to be known as super PACs—worked on behalf of both campaigns but their spending was far less than that of the two campaigns.

The idea that a candidate and his or her campaign would raise and spend most of the money in any race seems logical. It makes sense that candidates and their teams should be the dominant players in any election. But in key races around the country, that is becoming increasingly a rarity. Outside groups now routinely spend far more than candidates and their campaigns. This impacts both parties, but the greatest effect is within the Republican Party as it has abandoned its role as a center-right political party for an autocratic movement.

The 2022 Ohio and Arizona races for the U.S. Senate are perfect case studies of the rising power of the anti-democratic American *Siloviki*. J. D. Vance and Blake Masters were listed on the two states' respective ballots as Republicans, but they were really running on the Peter Thiel ticket.

"Fuck You World" and "A Strange, Strange Boy" are the titles of the first two chapters of Max Chafkin's book *The Contrarian: Peter Thiel and Silicon Valley's Pursuit of Power.* Those are followed by "Hope You Die," "World Domination Index," and "Heinous Activity." Had he not stumbled into making a fortune with PayPal, Thiel likely would simply be one of those oddball characters everyone remembers from high school or college—a loner who's angry and obsessed with being proven the smartest, the guy you feel vaguely bad about, wondering if his life might have worked out if you and your classmates had done more to make him feel accepted.

In 1995, before PayPal, Thiel cowrote a book attacking diversity on campus that included a passage about women and rape that could be lifted straight from *Incels for Dummies.* "But since a multicultural rape charge may indicate nothing more than belated regret, a woman might 'realize' that she had been 'raped' the next day or even many days later. Under these circumstances, it is unclear who should be held responsible. If the alcohol made both of them do it, then why should the woman's consent be obviated any more than the man's? Why is all blame placed on the man?"

As to what "multicultural rape" is versus any other kind of rape, it's hard not to conclude that what Thiel means is that some white Stanford coed might have sex with someone who was, say, Black, and then regret it and accuse her partner of rape. I suppose that's what he means, although it's difficult to get inside the mind of someone who is asking why men are more likely to be accused of rape than women.

Similar to his view of rape, Thiel developed views on government and democracy that were outside the mainstream. In a 2009 essay for the Cato Institute, a libertarian think tank funded largely by the Koch brothers, Thiel wrote:

I remain committed to the faith of my teenage years: to authentic human freedom as a precondition for the highest good. I stand against confiscatory taxes, totalitarian collectives, and the ideology of the inevitability of the death of every individual. But I must confess that over the last two decades, I have changed radically on the question of how to achieve these goals. Most importantly, I no longer believe that freedom and democracy are compatible.

The 1920s were the last decade in American history during which one could be genuinely optimistic about politics. Since 1920, the vast increase in welfare beneficiaries and the extension of the franchise to women—two constituencies that are notoriously tough for libertarians—have rendered the notion of "capitalist democracy" into an oxymoron.

This is, to be generous, nutty stuff. For Peter Thiel, death and taxes are not inevitable. "I believe if we could enable people to live forever, we should do that. I think this is absolute," Thiel told a *Washington Post* reporter in 2015, and he has spent millions to date funding research into anti-aging and life extension. To end the need for taxes, Thiel has also funded the development of floating cities in international waters known as "seasteading." The Seasteading Institute—yes, there is such a thing—says its goal is to "establish permanent, autonomous ocean communities to enable experimentation and innovation with diverse social, political, and legal systems." Thiel himself puts it bluntly: "The nature of government is about to change at a very fundamental level."

Presumably, on these island paradises, there will be no need for women to vote, although no one will be voting because Thiel doesn't believe in democracy. And until he can build his own tiny countries, Thiel will have to make do attempting to take over American politics. As Max Chafkin describes in *The Contrarian*:

Over the prior two decades, Peter Thiel had accumulated billions of dollars in wealth, backing some of the biggest and most successful tech companies, including Facebook, PayPal, and SpaceX. He'd built a network that gave him access to the best entrepreneurs and the wealthiest investors in the world, and he was idolized by a generation of aspiring startup founders. But Thiel wanted more than sway in Silicon Valley—he wanted real power, political power.

Thiel had long been a mentor to Mark Zuckerberg, who began Facebook at Harvard as Facemash, an online site where men could rate female classmates, a version of what was commonly known as a "Pig Book." Thiel was an original board member of Facebook and its first outside investor. As he developed a public image as an Obama-friendly supporter of immigration reform, "Zuckerberg had continued to rely on Thiel as a liaison to the American right. Thiel, according to Zuckerberg's allies, was the company's conservative conscience," Chafkin writes. "Zuckerberg's critics saw Thiel's influence on the company as more profound—and more pernicious. He was, in this view, the puppet master: pushing a younger, ideologically uncertain founder toward an alliance with an extremist wing of the Republican Party."

That alliance was created on May 18, 2016. On that day, the political media's attention was focused on Donald Trump's big win in the Oregon Republican primary, but it's quite likely that the 2016 presidential election was actually decided on May 18 in a meeting at Facebook headquarters in Menlo Park, California. Responding to attacks from the right that Facebook was censoring conservative voices, Thiel facilitated a meeting of sixteen prominent right-wing figures, Zuckerberg, and himself. The gathering included Fox News's Tucker Carlson and the loony Glenn Beck, the presidents of the Tea Party Patriots, the American Enterprise Institute, and the Heritage Foundation. Max Chafkin describes the outcome:

> Facebook intended to allow supporters of Donald Trump, who was by then the de facto Republican nominee, to say more or less whatever they wanted on its platform. Over the next several months, misinformation on Facebook—much of it in Trump's favor—outperformed real news. The most popular election headline on Facebook during that period, according to one study, was "Pope Francis Shocks the World, Endorses Donald Trump for President," which, of course, never happened. Another claimed falsely that Wikileaks emails revealed that Hillary Clinton had sold weapons to Islamic State terrorists.

In that one meeting, two American oligarchs, Peter Thiel and Mark Zuckerberg, exercised more political power than any Russian billionaire. It was a classic example of the autocrats' playbook to utilize the tolerances of democracy to attack democracy. Later, Zuckerberg would feign ignorance of the impact of his decision on the election, telling Congress, "We didn't take a broad enough view of our responsibility, and that was a big mistake." He uttered those words with the sincerity of a hostage statement, using the undefined "we" to spread blame—this from the man who once had business cards that read, "I'm CEO...bitch."

Peter Thiel was rewarded with a speaking slot at the Republican National Convention. And when Americans learned that Trump had bragged about assaulting women with the release of the *Access Hollywood* tape, Thiel's reaction was to donate $1.25 million to super PACs supporting Trump. The angry young man who wrote a book accusing women of falsely claiming "multicultural rape" was now a billionaire with the ability to help elect a man credibly accused of over twenty cases of sexual assault. After the election, Thiel was given an office in Trump Tower.

Following Donald Trump's defeat by Joe Biden in 2020, after the attack on the Capitol on January 6, 2021, and after the Republican Party adopted the Big Lie that America no longer had a legally elected president, Peter Thiel looked out at the American landscape and decided the problem with the Republican Party was that it was too moderate. His solution was to recruit and fund his own candidates in two critical senate races, Arizona and Ohio. His choice for candidates were two men who had worked for him and he had made wealthy at a young age: J. D. Vance in Ohio and Blake Masters in Arizona.

Neither one had ever run for office before and had little support among voters, even within the Republican Party. Under federal campaign finance limits, Peter Thiel could donate no more than $5,800 to any candidate running for federal office—$2,900 in the primary and $2,900 in the general election. But it was perfectly legal for him to pour $30 million into a super PAC supporting Masters and Vance.

Any American can fund a super PAC to support any federal candidate of their choice. There are plenty of ultra-wealthy individuals on the left who pour vast sums into politics. George Soros, for example, contributed $175 million through his PAC to Democratic candidates exclusively, making him the largest donor during the 2022 midterms.

But what makes the influence of a Peter Thiel far more powerful is the collapse of the Republican Party. Michael Bloomberg, Michael Eisner, Sam Bankman-Fried, Fred Eychaner, and many more can and do help elect Democratic candidates, some more to the left than others. But once elected, the candidates they support exist within the boundaries of a functioning political party that is still in the American mainstream. With the backing of Peter Thiel, Blake Masters and J. D. Vance had no obligation, need, or desire to conform to the norms of either their state or national parties. Once they'd secured the nomination, those parties needed their support more than they needed the support of the party. Before getting in the race, the candidates had won the most important contest—the Peter Thiel primary—by demonstrating their loyalty to Thiel, being reliant on Thiel for financial security, and an ability to fit into the world of misogynist oddballs whom Thiel had elevated since his days at Stanford.

It's difficult to know what's real and what's not about a curious character like J. D. Vance. The question of what happened to him has become something of a cottage industry, with hundreds of observers trying to figure out how a once seemingly reasonable human being like Vance could transform into the caricature of a rabid Trump supporter. But my take on J. D. Vance, just like my view of Lindsey Graham, is that he likely didn't change at all. The rise of Trump simply made it possible in multiple ways for Vance to reveal who he always was, without any need to pretend.

The Lindsey Grahams and J. D. Vances are motivated by a deep personal grievance that, when combined with a desperate ambition, removes any of the concerns a normal person would have about appearing to have lived much of their lives as a lie. But on one important level, it doesn't matter what is going on inside of J. D. Vance. What matters is that Vance is useful to a character like Peter Thiel.

It would be impossible for a Democratic Senate candidate to encourage women to stay in violent marriages without being rebuked by the state or the national party and losing support among Democratic voters. Any such statement would be seen as completely violating the basic values of the Democratic Party. But J. D. Vance, whose entire candidacy was made possible by the man who wrote about women regretting "multicultural" sex and later calling it rape, has no such problems. In an October 2022 interview, Vance said:

> This is one of the great tricks that I think the sexual revolution pulled on the American populace, which is the idea that like, "well, OK, these marriages were fundamentally, you know, they were maybe even violent, but certainly they were unhappy. And so, getting rid of them and making it easier for people to shift spouses like they change their underwear, that's going to make people happier in the long term."

When asked about his opposition to abortion, even in cases of rape and incest, Vance referred to rape as "inconvenient." "It's not whether a woman should be forced to bring a child to term; it's whether a child should be allowed to live, even though the circumstances of that child's birth are somehow inconvenient or a problem to the society." Rape as "inconvenient" is not an official Republican position but it does read as if it was lifted from Peter Thiel's *The Diversity Myth*. And Vance received no blow-back whatsoever from the party for his inconvenient rape theory.

A functioning political party will include different views and the diversity of those opinions can be a great strength. But there will be lines that cannot be crossed and still maintain the support of the party. Calling rape "inconvenient" should be unacceptable for any candidate in any party. But if your candidacy is funded by a single deep-pocket donor who supports your positions, all the guardrails are removed.

That still doesn't remove a candidate from the scrutiny of voters. Peter Thiel can't force anyone to vote for one of his candidates, but his influence becomes far greater—and his likelihood of winning skyrockets—when he is promoting the candidates of a party that has abandoned any role in upholding accepted norms. He has no need or desire to pretend that his efforts are to participate in a democracy and has stated clearly he does not support democracy.

It would be reasonable to assume that Peter Thiel would feel deep gratitude for the American system, one that enabled him to amass great wealth. No other country in the world would have offered a "strange, strange boy"—as Thiel was described by one of his early teachers—the opportunity to legally amass great wealth and power at a very young age. But instead of expressing gratitude, Thiel's reaction is to spend a fortune undermining that very system. Instead of trying to strengthen democracy and celebrating basic values like women's suffrage as an essential pillar of the system, Thiel uses the freedom sustained by the system to elect candidates who share his goal of destroying the system.

In Arizona, the Thiel candidate was Blake Masters, who had caught Thiel's attention when he was a student in a class called Startups that Thiel taught at Stanford. Masters published online accounts of Thiel's classes that bring to mind what the Gospels would have been like if written by libertarian, CrossFit-loving Stanford students eager to get very wealthy very fast. Later Masters, when running for the Senate as Thiel's candidate, named Ted Kaczynski as a "subversive thinker that's underrated." For some, having a protégé who also admired the Unabomber might have been troubling, but apparently not for Peter Thiel.

Working as coauthors, Masters and Thiel transformed Masters's class notes into a bestselling business book, *Zero to One*. Then, Thiel hired Masters as chief operating officer of his investment firm Thiel Capital and president of the Thiel Foundation. In March 2022, Masters resigned from those positions so he could run for the Arizona Senate seat held by former astronaut Mark Kelly, the husband of former Tucson-area Congresswoman Gabby Giffords, who had very nearly been assassinated in 2011.

Like J. D. Vance in Ohio, Masters had had no previous

involvement in Arizona politics. He had lived in California since he'd left to attend Stanford and had had no real
connection with the state of Arizona since his high school
days at an elite private school. Without Thiel's backing, he
would have been dead on arrival as a candidate. But Thiel's
money instantly made him a very viable one, and Masters
soon drew Donald Trump's endorsement.

The combination pushed Masters over the top, and he
won the Republican nomination to face incumbent Senator Mark Kelly. The contrast could not have been starker:
an astronaut and former fighter pilot who had fought to
defend democracy versus the maladjusted nerd who had
written that America "hasn't been involved in a just war
in over 140 years," in an online post that concluded with
a quote from Nazi leader Hermann Goering: "The people
can always be brought to the bidding of the leaders." Masters shared Thiel's view that democracy was a fatally flawed
form of government. "I'd rather have fewer people vote, but
have those votes be informed and intelligent, than just more
people." Masters said in a 2021 interview, "We need less
people voting, not more."

Masters emerged as one of the stranger candidates in the
2022 midterms, a significant achievement in a year in which
former vampire porn actress Tudor Dixon was the Republican nominee for governor in Michigan. At Stanford, he
had posted a series of shirtless videos on Bodybuilding.com

to chronicle his unsuccessful efforts to develop a body that didn't scream pocket-protector nerd. Continuing Thiel's assault on what he called political correctness, and what most people call simple decency, Masters shot a rap video of himself at Stanford in face paint mocking Native Americans. So it was not surprising, if still bizarre, when his campaign released a series of videos of Masters in the desert expressing a fetishist love of guns. In one, he erotically caresses a silenced Walther PPK handgun, a weapon Ian Fleming had issued to his James Bond character. "I've wanted this gun a long time. Ever since I was a little kid. Made in Germany. Double-O Seven gun. Why would you not want this?" The total effect was a mix of the sort of videos school shooters post before leaving home for the last time and an audition tape for a fetish film.

Arizonans voted 51.4 percent to 46.5 percent for the astronaut over the weirdo in the desert with guns, but that still meant that 1.2 million people voted for a candidate whose sole qualification was that he was Peter Thiel's Mini-Me. Had Thiel picked an Arizona candidate who identified more as a normal person and less as a kind of Zodiac Killer lite, he would have elected two senators who shared his anti-democratic views in key presidential swing states instead of only one. The Republican National Committee's reaction to Masters's defeat was to appoint him to a commission whose nominal mission was to study why

Republicans underperformed in the 2022 midterms, a move akin to a restaurant chain asking Jeffrey Dahmer to advise on declining sales.

There is a strange and perplexing irony to the funding of the anti-democratic movement in America. Like Peter Thiel, the 1 percent of the 1 percent of the wealthiest Americans funding anti-democratic efforts are those who not only have benefited the most from democratic capitalism but who also potentially have the most to lose in an autocratic system. Autocrats like Donald Trump and Ron DeSantis are eager to use the power of the state to punish powerful interests in the business world. "With all of the Fake News coming out of NBC and the Networks, at what point is it appropriate to challenge their License? Bad for country," Trump tweeted, causing a drop in the share price of NBC's parent company, Comcast.

In Florida, Governor Ron DeSantis launched an attack on Disney when they refused to support his legislation limiting the discussion of sexual orientation in schools. A governor attacking the Happiness Company in Florida, a state in which tourism is its foundational industry, seems both deranged and self-defeating. But for DeSantis, the negative impact on his state is inconsequential if he can score points with the homophobic base of the Republican Party. "If Disney wants to pick a fight, they chose the wrong guy," DeSantis boasted in a fundraising email. Only in today's

Republican Party could taking on Tinkerbell be seen as bolstering your Tough Guy credentials. Disney responded by canceling a billion-dollar expansion in Florida that would have brought thousands of jobs. Tinkerbell won.

Of course, a powerful government official trying to bully a business to suit his political agenda is antithetical to conservatism. But Republican leaders like DeSantis aren't conservative. They are autocrats unhindered by the principles of any governing philosophy. DeSantis is not from the business world. His only job in the private sector was a short stint teaching high school history at a private school in Georgia, nine months he rather curiously avoids mentioning. Looking at a list of his many corporate donors, I have to wonder do they not realize they support a man who will do everything he can to punish them if they dare disagree or oppose his agenda?

There is an unwillingness and inability among many in the donor class to adjust to the reality that they are supporting elected officials who are trying to kill democracy in America. On January 6, 2021, 65 percent of the Republicans in the House of Representatives, joined by eight Republican senators, voted not to certify the November election for president. There's no reason to believe it won't be a much higher percentage following the next election if, once more, a Republican fails to win.

There is no more fundamental assault on democracy and

the rule of law than overturning the results of a free and fair election. Prior to the January 6 insurrection, 280 Fortune 500 companies had donated to the 147 senators and members of Congress who voted not to certify the election. Following the coup attempt, CNN reached out to those companies to ask if they would continue to fund the campaigns of the pro-insurrectionists. Of those who responded, 120 said they had decided to pause or end donations. "This was a free and fair election," Hewlett-Packard said in a statement. "Any attempt to overturn the will of voters is a threat to our democracy. HP's Political Action Committee did not make any contributions during this cycle to members who voted against the certification of the presidential election results."

Two years later, HP's political action committee donated to four incumbents who had voted not to certify the election. Over half the companies who had pledged to discontinue donations quietly resumed their support. More than $10 million in corporate money went to campaigns of officeholders who voted not to certify the 2020 election.

———

As dangerous as the specter of Republicans in Washington refusing to certify the next presidential election, the most threatening anti-democratic candidates are actually those who have run and will run in the future for governor. Governors have tremendous power over state elections, particularly if they are willing to break norms and exert that power. In Pennsylvania, State Senator Doug Mastriano ran for governor in 2022, making Trump's Big Lie the centerpiece of his campaign. Mastriano spent campaign funds to charter a bus to take protestors to the January 6 Trump rally and later was questioned by the FBI about his role. Despite Biden winning the state by 80,555 votes, Mastriano continued to claim Trump won Pennsylvania.

Calling it "election reform," Mastriano pledged sweeping changes to Pennsylvania's voting laws, including ending "no excuses" voting by mail in that state, which allows any individual to vote by simply mailing in a ballot. Mastriano's "reform" would force all voters to re-register, something that would be a violation of federal law. Because Pennsylvania is one of only fifteen states whose secretary of state is appointed by the governor, Mastriano made it clear that he would choose a chief election officer who shared his draconian views. "The most important thing is I get to appoint the Secretary of State and that Secretary of State is going to clean up the election laws," Mastriano boasted. "We're going to reset, in fact, registration. You're going to have to re-register. We're going to start all over again....I saw better elections in Afghanistan than I saw in Pennsylvania."

In Arizona, Kari Lake, who campaigned for governor on a similar Big Lie platform, has refused to concede and never will, despite losing by over 17,000 votes. She's using denial of her defeat as an audition to run as the vice-presidential running mate of another loser, Donald Trump, or in a 2024 Senate race.

At its heart, the Big Lie is a direct attack on American civil society. Every dollar that goes to support Republicans who refuse to accept that Joe Biden won a free and fair election is undermining American democracy. It is democracy's version of 9/11 Truthers, who claim the attacks were a government plot. For a movement that considers itself right-wing and conservative, the Big Lie ironically mirrors the century-long attacks on American democracy by the Soviet Union. Beginning in the 1920s, the Soviet propaganda machine alleged that America was an oligarchy of wealthy white men who believed in racism and financial inequality. One hundred years later, Russian attacks on America remain unchanged. The Russian strategy to help elect Donald Trump in 2016 was focused on an attempt to undermine belief in the American political system. The 2019 Mueller report—officially titled *Report on the Investigation into Russian Interference in the 2016 Presidential Election*—insists that Russia's covert "Internet Research Agency" undoubtedly "conducted social media operations targeted at large U.S. audiences with the goal of sowing discord in the U.S. political system."

"Sowing discord in the U.S. political system" is precisely the message at the core of the autocratic movement. That's what Doug Mastriano is doing when he says, "We're going to start all over again." That's what Kari Lake is doing when she says, "I won this election, and everybody knows it."

It's easy to focus on the loudest and most strident of the election deniers who are trying hard to destroy faith in democracy, but Lake and Mastriano were only two of twenty-two Republican candidates for governor in 2022 who ran for office in a country they claim does not have a legal president. Once, this would have been considered not only disqualifying but also just plain loony, yet now it is the mainstream position in the Republican Party. It is a fundamental rejection of the rule of law, and it would be reasonable to expect the American business community, which is dependent on laws to function and flourish, would unite in opposition.

But many of the leading corporations in this country routinely send large amounts of money to the Republican Governors Association, which endorsed a full slate of election-denying candidates in 2022. (In 2020, the top twenty corporate donors contributed a combined $17,342,721 to the RGA.) Each of these publicly held corporations would consider it absurd to suggest they oppose democracy. They spend billions on advertising and public relations to cultivate American mainstream images and assert that they hold dear the best American values. But by continuing to support an organization dedicated to electing and reelecting governors who don't believe America is a functioning democracy, they are complicit in helping destroy democracy.

This is part of the larger failure of much of corporate America to accept the truth that there is nothing normal about this moment in American politics. In my 2020 book *It Was All a Lie*, I insist that Trump didn't change the Republican Party—he revealed it. He was a natural evolution of the combination of white grievance and ambition-absent-principle that had become dominant within the party. But since publishing that in 2020, I have watched the party accelerate its move to autocracy. Today, it requires an act of great and deliberate delusion to ignore the threat to democracy held by the Republican Party. Yet corporate donors continue to feed the beast that is eating the free enterprise system in which they have flourished. Supporting a political organization like the Republican Governors Association was once an ideological and plainly practical decision that many corporate donors found both appealing and productive. That can no longer be true when the majority of the Republican governors refuse to acknowledge that President Biden is our legally elected president.

It didn't have to be this way.

In the 1991 Louisiana governor's race, former KKK Grand Wizard David Duke ran against former Democratic Governor Edwin Edwards. Louisiana has an open primary system where all candidates run on the same ballot, and if no candidate receives 50 percent of the vote, the top two finishers, regardless of party, go into a runoff to determine the winner. Duke did not run as a Republican. But because he faced the former Democratic governor, he was seen as the de facto Republican alternative. Duke even dubbed himself "the Republican candidate." Duke maintained he had undergone a Christian conversion and asked for forgiveness and a chance at redemption.

The Republican Governors Association not only refused to support Duke, but organized an effort to defeat him that was led by former Republican Governor Dave Treen. In that role, Treen was helping elect the man who had defeated him when he ran for reelection in 1983—Edwin Edwards. President George W. Bush attacked Duke, saying, "When someone asserts the Holocaust never took place, then I don't believe that person ever deserves one iota of public trust. When someone has so recently endorsed Nazism, it is inconceivable that someone can reasonably aspire to a leadership role in a free society."

Today the leader of the Republican Party meets with a white supremacist holocaust denier, Nick Fuentes, and outrage is replaced by silence or approval

In her brilliant 2016 book *Dark Money*, Jane Mayer details the decades-long efforts by a few powerful families to push American politics and culture to the right, featuring the strange odyssey of the Koch family. As Mayer tells it, the story of the Koch family is a uniquely American one. The sweep and ambition, and tragedy, depicted in *Citizen Kane* is a perfect model for the lives of the four Koch brothers. It's a story that begins with vast inherited wealth of dubious origin, a fortune made by a domineering father who helped both Stalin and Hitler develop the oil industries critical to their war efforts. In 1938, Fred Koch wrote to a friend extolling the virtues of what soon would be the Axis powers. "Although nobody agrees with me, I am of the opinion that the only sound countries in the world are Germany, Italy, and Japan, simply because they are all working and working hard."

The four brothers were raised in the very normal setting of Wichita, Kansas, in a very abnormal home. Wealthy at an early age from his oil-refining business, their father married a beautiful Wellesley socialite and went about constructing a life that was more *Great Gatsby* than Kansas heartland, one that included a massive home described as "baronial," with the mounted heads of exotic animals shot on African safari, polo ponies, and a German governess who was a great admirer of Hitler. There was almost nothing about the formative years of the four Koch brothers that could be considered part of the American mainstream.

The German nanny returned to the Fatherland to celebrate when Hitler conquered France, but before leaving, she subjected the boys to the sort of treatment you might expect of a Nazi-loving disciplinarian. "She enforced a rigid toilet-training regimen requiring the boys to produce morning bowel movements precisely on schedule or be force-fed castor oil and subjected to enemas," Mayer writes. The father loved to see the boys competing against each other, staging boxing matches, and was quick to enforce his rules with brutal whippings.

Predictably, by the time they were adults, the boys had become four very wealthy, maladjusted brothers who developed political views as unusual as their upbringing. The oldest, Frederick—the defendant in a mock trial the younger brothers held to determine if he was gay—distanced himself from the family and moved to France. Following their father's death, the remaining three brothers engaged in vicious litigation against each other over control of the Koch empire, a battle that was finally settled with the two middle brothers, Charles and David, winning control of the company while Bill—younger than his twin brother, David, by nineteen minutes—dedicated himself to sailing, and collecting everything from art to military hardware.

Despite being the beneficiaries of an economic system that allowed them to inherit and amass unimaginable wealth, Charles and David Koch have spent their lives trying to radically alter the fundamental role of government in the United States. Heavily influenced by their father's tales of the oppressive role of the state in Stalin's Russia, where he helped build oil refineries, Charles and David Koch also became enamored of the Austrian school of economics led by Friedrich Hayek, who won the Nobel Prize for Economics in 1974. As Christopher Leonard describes in *Kochland*:

> In Hayek's view, even well-intentioned state actions ended up causing far more human suffering than the market-based ills that they were meant to correct. Hayek was almost religious when it came to describing what the market could do when left to its own devices. He believed that the market was more important, and more beneficial, than the institution of democracy itself. A market was able to mediate all the wishes of everyone on earth. Laws and regulations were unworthy tools to use to deal with problems of the natural world, because the natural world was always changing. Laws were static; the world was fluid. Only the market could respond to the ways the world rapidly changed, Hayek believed.

Hayek is the patron saint of the Libertarian movement, and in many ways the Libertarian Party in America became a natural home for the Kochs. In 1980, David Koch ran for vice president on the Libertarian ticket and donated more than $2 million to the party, a huge amount for a political organization that was little more than a loose affiliation of oddball intellectuals and anti-government cranks. The 1980 Libertarian Party manifesto reads as if much of it could have been written by Ted Kaczynski:

> We, the members of the Libertarian Party, challenge the cult of the omnipotent state and defend the rights of the individual. We hold that all individuals have the right to exercise sole dominion over their own lives and have the right to live in whatever manner they choose, so long as they do not forcibly interfere with the equal right of others to live in whatever manner they choose. Governments throughout history have regularly operated on the opposite principle— the notion that the state has the right to dispose of the lives of individuals and the fruits of their labor. Even within the United States, all political parties other than our own grant to government the right to regulate the lives of individuals and seize the fruits of their labor without their consent.

From that unusual opening gambit, the platform only got nuttier. Libertarians called for the abolishment of the Food and Drug Administration; the Department of Energy; the Environmental Protection Agency; the Nuclear Regulatory Commission; the Federal Aviation Administration; the

Bureau of Land Management; the Federal Election Commission; the Bureau of Alcohol, Tobacco and Firearms; and the Federal Trade Commission. They also called for the repeal of the Occupational Safety and Health Act, and they opposed gun regulations of any sort.

The 1980 Libertarian campaign that featured David Koch as the party's vice-presidential candidate advocated the repeal of Social Security, Medicare, and Medicaid. It called for an end to all federal speed limits and for the privatization of public schools, railroads, highways, and all public lands. No more national parks. Years later, anti-tax crusader Grover Norquist infamously quipped, "My goal is to cut government in half in twenty-five years, to get it down to the size where we can drown it in the bathtub." But that statement would have pegged him as a pro–big government liberal by David Koch's Libertarian standards.

Running as the vice-presidential candidate on a Libertarian presidential ticket was a harmless indulgence, like kids playing with toy guns. But in the decades that followed, the Koch brothers methodically and relentlessly pursued their unique visions of American governance and civil society with the same organizational brilliance and opportunism that has made their company, Koch Industries, an integral, if often unseen, part of our lives. Leonard describes the vast scope of the business in *Kochland*:

It specialized in the kind of businesses that are indispensable to modern civilization but which most consumers never directly encounter. The company is embedded in the hidden infrastructure of everyday life. Millions of people use Koch's products without ever seeing Koch's name attached. Koch refines and distributes fossil fuels, from gasoline to jet fuel, on which the global economy is dependent. Koch is the world's third largest producer of nitrogen fertilizer, which is the cornerstone of the modern food system. Koch makes the synthetic materials used in baby diapers, waistbands, and carpets. It makes the chemicals used for plastic bottles and pipes. It owns Georgia-Pacific, which makes the wall panels, beams, and plywood required to build homes and office buildings. It makes napkins, paper towels, stationery, newspaper, and personal hygiene products.

This was the approach the Koch brothers took to American politics. They infiltrated the right-wing political infrastructure at every level. They funded the Cato Institute, a libertarian think tank, and the conservative Heritage Foundation to help create a policy framework easily adopted by Republican candidates and lawmakers, many of whom ran with little knowledge of government or a basic ability to articulate an agenda other than offer bromides like "smaller government, less regulation, lower taxes."

Through various organizations—some directly political, supporting candidates and some operating as charitable foundations promoting "issue advocacy"—the Kochs built a vast network that functioned as both its own political party and shadow government. By 2015, they had 1,200 full-time staffers in over one hundred offices around the country, three and a half times more employees than the Republican National Committee. They recruited candidates, financed their campaigns, and provided policy support and opposition research on their opponents. Preparing for the 2016 campaign, they had plans to back a candidate for the Republican nomination, then do everything possible to elect that candidate president. Their anticipated budget was slightly under a billion dollars.

But then Trump happened. In August 2015, the Koch brothers—under the umbrella of Freedom Partners, one of their political organizations—invited potential Republican primary candidates to address the group in what was called "the Koch primary." Meeting in Orange County, California, the favorites for the Koch endorsement were former Florida Governor Jeb Bush, Florida Senator Marco Rubio, Texas Senator Ted Cruz, Wisconsin Governor Scott Walker, and the former CEO of HP, Carly Fiorina. Each had answered a detailed questionnaire prior to the meeting. Donald Trump was an announced candidate in August 2015—but he was not invited.

As befitted their deep belief in the power of the market, the Kochs intended to wait awhile before making a formal endorsement of one candidate. "Only if somebody really stands out from the standpoint of their message," Charles Koch said, "and what they would actually do to benefit America and has a decent chance of being elected, only then would we select one over the others."

By February, six months later, the market had spoken. Donald Trump was cruising his way to the Republican nomination and the Kochs did not yet have a candidate.

Trump, in fact, was everything the Koch brothers hated. Long advocates for liberal immigration policies that are good for providing workers for businesses, Charles Koch said of Trump's call for a Muslim ban, "That's reminiscent of Nazi Germany. I mean, that's monstrous." Instead of privatizing Social Security and Medicare, the Koch goal for decades, Trump defended both as federal necessities and attacked Republicans. Prior to the primary in Wisconsin, home of Congressman Paul Ryan, who had long advocated privatization, Trump said in an interview:

> You know, Paul wants to knock out Social Security, knock it down, way down. He wants to knock

Medicare way down. And frankly, well, two things. Number one, you're going to lose the election if you're going to do that. That's going to be easy. I'm not going to cut it, and I'm not going to raise ages, and I'm not going to do all of the things that they want to do. But they want to really cut it, and they want to cut it very substantially, the Republicans, and I'm not going to do that.

That was a long way from the Libertarian platform Charles Koch ran on in 1980. The Kochs were pressured to support Trump, but they refused. "It is hard for me to get a high level of enthusiasm because the things I'm passionate about and I think this country urgently needs aren't being addressed," Koch said in an interview in the *Financial Times*. But when asked by ABC's Jonathan Karl if he planned to help with the "Never Trump" movement, Charles Koch answered negatively. When pressed why, he said, "Because that's not what we do. What we're trying to do is build alliances to make the country better."

The Koch brothers hold positions outside the American political norm, but their libertarian vision is antithetical to an autocracy. By definition, autocracies exert tremendous power over the governed, reward loyalty over merit, and control markets based on political favoritism. But after spending billions of dollars and erecting the most powerful private political organization in U.S. history, the Kochs seemed powerless to steer the Republican Party away from Donald Trump. They watched while many of the operatives they had groomed helped elect a man they loathed.

It was a scene straight out of science fiction: the machine turned on its creators. The Kochs had political principles. The vast army they created had none. And Mike Pence was the living embodiment of how the Kochs' power was exploited as a weapon to attack what they had hoped to accomplish.

There would never have been a Vice President Mike Pence were it not for the Koch brothers. David Koch gave more money to Mike Pence's campaigns than he had to any other politician, over $300,000 to help elect him governor of Indiana. Pence was effectively created in the Kochs' laboratory. He had run for Congress twice and lost. In his second campaign, he had been caught paying his mortgage with campaign funds, an FEC violation. Now a disgraced losing candidate, he was rescued by a job offer from the Koch-backed local think tank called the Indiana Policy Review. He used that position to host a radio show he dubbed "Rush Limbaugh on decaf."

When he was eventually elected to Congress in 2000, Pence's chief of staff was Marc Short, who later became president of the Kochs' Freedom Partners. Pence's congressional press aide, Matt Lloyd, became communications director for Koch Industries. As governor, Pence signed the Koch-authored pledge not to support any taxes on carbon emissions aimed at fighting global warming. When Pence's broad tax-cutting agenda was at risk, the Koch organization Americans for Prosperity stepped in to help.

At a 2014 Dallas event called Defending the American Dream, organized by the largest Koch political apparatus, Americans for Prosperity, Pence paid tribute to their help. "The reason I got on that airplane and am standing before all of you today...is to say thanks simply." Pence described how the Indiana chapter of Americans for Prosperity helped when his tax cut was stalled. "AFP of Indiana, at a critical moment in that debate, came alongside our administration and informed the people of Indiana. And we put together an income tax cut and a tax-cut package that was the largest state tax cut in Indiana history. And AFP made a difference."

When Pence became vice president, Koch staffer Marc Short again became his chief of staff. Although Trump was definitely not their guy, it would have been impossible to imagine the Kochs having a more powerful ally in Washington than Vice President Pence. But it didn't matter. Pence didn't change Donald Trump; he served Donald Trump.

When he was offered the chance to run with Trump, Pence did what the Republican Party did, making it plain that he cared about nothing but power. After decades of every imaginable kind of support from the Kochs, Mike

Pence, the Christian evangelical, jumped at the chance to support the man who talked in public about having sex with his daughter, increased the deficit more than any president in history, abolished NAFTA, supported tariffs, attacked immigrants, and tried to overthrow the results of a presidential election.

When he became aware of plans for a coup attempt on January 6, 2021, Pence didn't call the FBI or inform the public. He called Dan Quayle to see if it was possible to violate his constitutional oath. At the last minute, when it was clear the coup would fail, he threw in with the winning side.

The Kochs also groomed others who assumed key positions in the Trump administration. Trump's CIA head was Kansas Congressman Mike Pompeo, who had received so much money from the Kochs that he was known as the "Congressman from Koch." A lobbyist for Koch was head of the Trump transition "energy independence team." And the watchdog group Public Citizen reported that "forty-four Trump administration officials have close ties to the Koch brothers and their political groups."

Trump himself dealt with the Kochs the way autocrats always maneuver their potential adversaries. He didn't fight them; he co-opted them, giving them enough of what they wanted to neutralize any possible opposition from them. It was exactly the way in which Hungarian dictator Viktor Orbán had consolidated power. "This form of soft dictatorship does not require mass violence to stay in power," Anne Applebaum writes in *Twilight of Democracy.* "Instead, it relies upon a cadre of elites to run the bureaucracy, the state media, the courts, and, in some places, state companies."

The Kochs could have used their political empire to rally a primary challenge to Trump in 2020, but they did not. Instead, they publicly declared that they were staying out of the presidential race. "The conservative Koch political network has told donors that it plans to once again stay out of the presidential race and will not work to help reelect President Trump in 2020," the *Washington Post* reported, calling it "a move that sidelines a major player that has been pivotal in mobilizing voters on the right for more than a decade."

But, in fact, the Kochs did help Trump in his 2020 campaign. The claim that their refusal to back Trump "sidelines a major player" is false. By backing Republican senatorial and congressional candidates in key races around the country, they were helping Trump, even if that was not their avowed intent. Without Koch financial assistance to downticket Republican candidates, Trump would have lost by an even larger margin.

While Donald Trump the presidential candidate lost in 2020, Trumpism is now the driving force of the Republican Party, a classic tale of the law of unintended consequences. After decades during which the Kochs built the most sophisticated political operation in the history of the country, the center-right party in America is now much farther away from its stated small-government goals than when the Koch brothers first began their efforts to remake American governance. The men and women they helped elect, the Mike Pences sprinkled across the country, are now all supporters of Trumpism. Some are more enthusiastic than others, but there is no credible anti-Trump movement in the Republican Party. The Libertarian-loving Kochs unwittingly have become the largest financers by far of an autocratic American movement that embodies much of what they fear and loathe about government.

To stop the big government threat they feared, the Kochs backed Republicans, assuming they could control the direction of the party. By living in the fantasy world that they could support Republican candidates other than Trump and not support Trumpism, they have enabled Trumpism to grow.

David Koch died in 2019, leaving Charles Koch in charge of the political operation. And there is tacit acknowledgment within the Koch political world that all of it has gone badly wrong. Americans for Prosperity released a blunt memo following the 2022 midterms that acknowledged the bleak Kochian landscape. "The Republican Party is nominating bad candidates who are advocating for things that go against core American principles," the memo stated. "And the American people are rejecting them. The Democratic Party increasingly sees this as a political opportunity. And they're responding with more and more extreme policies, policies that also go against our core American principles." Eight years after Trump's emergence, the Koch organizations are finally acknowledging the reality of what the Republican Party has become. But it's difficult to imagine that even the Kochs have the ability to change the direction of the party. If they support candidates who run to "save" the party from Trumpism, those candidates will lose. Their party is now occupied by a hostile power, and like the Norwegians and French of post-German invasion, they are in the morally compromised position of negotiating with evil.

Eight years after Trump emerged, there is a painful and sad irony at the heart of America's movement to autocracy. Much of the financial base of the party of Trumpism is opposed to what Trumpism is doing to American politics. But for all their financial power, they are unwilling to do what is necessary to cure the cancer that is threatening the system in which they have thrived. So it will continue to spread. They are yet to acknowledge that even when they elect one of their own, like Virginia Governor Glenn Youngkin, the former CEO of the Carlyle Group, the Harvard MBA alum of McKinsey & Company, he will do what it takes to advance in the party of Trumpism. It's a pathetic spectacle when Glenn Youngkin goes to Arizona to campaign for Kari Lake, a woman who supported the wildest of election conspiracy theories and wakes up every day attacking rule of law. Glenn Youngkin did not change Kari Lake. But Kari Lake changed Glenn Youngkin, making him complicit in the ongoing effort to destabilize our civil society.

This will continue until it no longer can. Campaigns never end because they want to; they end because they lose, or they run out of money. As long as the money continues to support the party that has adopted Trumpism, it will only grow more powerful. No anti-democratic movement becomes more democratic once in power.

Chapter 4

The Legal Theories

Whenever anybody starts telling you that they're worried about our democracy or protect our democracy, or they've got a democracy in their name, those are not friends of ours.

—Cleta Mitchell, former Donald Trump lawyer,
speaking to a Republican National Committee
donor group in 2023

I celebrated the night it all started to go wrong. That was December 12, 2000, when the *Bush v. Gore* decision came down from the Supreme Court.

I had moved to Austin in the spring of 1999 to work on the Bush campaign, and when Bush was declared the new president a year and a half later, I wasn't so much happy as relieved. Presidential campaigns are exhausting like no experience in politics, and while I wanted to win with the heat of a thousand suns, I wouldn't have feared for the country if we had lost.

Mostly, I was just tired and glad it was over and happy for all my friends with whom I'd spent eighteen months and experienced all the emotional ups and downs that are uniquely intense in a presidential campaign. In years since, when people have asked me about the Supreme Court's role in the 2000 election and the *Bush v. Gore* decision, I've just shrugged. And that was pretty much how I reacted at the end of every race I worked on, presidential or otherwise. It was over; I wanted to move on and focus on the next race.

In those days, I never thought much about the consequences

of the work I did for candidates. It was my job to win. If they won, I was happy. If not, I was miserable. Once elected, they were on their own. That was the stuff they called "governing," and it held little interest for me. I was a campaign guy. "Going inside," as we called working for a candidate you helped elect, had no appeal for me. Get up every morning to help him or her govern? I couldn't imagine anything more boring.

When Donald Trump emerged, I refused to believe my party would embrace his toxic blend of racism, xenophobia, and misogyny. It was unimaginable to me that someone who so clearly had no respect for the basic functions of democratic society, from elections to the judiciary, could be nominated by the Republican Party. Then, when he was, I remained in denial until about 10:00 p.m. on election night.

During the general-election campaign, I had spoken out against Trump, and each time I did, my phone would fill up with text messages from Republican elected officials and operatives thanking me. I didn't want to be praised; I wanted them to join in speaking out. There was nothing I was doing that they couldn't do but I got it. I knew how the game was played. After Trump had lost, they would all breathe a sigh of relief and say they were against him from the start.

On election night 2016, I was on a PBS election-coverage panel with Judy Woodruff, and as I stared at the results in disbelief, I suddenly began to receive a flood of messages from those same Republicans asking me to delete their previous messages discussing the disaster that was Donald Trump. At first, I thought they were joking. But as I watched these same people profess their admiration for President-elect Trump in the days ahead, I was struck with a growing sense of sadness, disappointment, and anger. I felt sad and disappointed about the party for which I had worked for decades and the fellow Republicans I witnessed debasing themselves in lies. But the anger I felt was self-directed. How did I not see this before?

I began to ask myself how I had so thoroughly misjudged many of my old friends and our party. The question of why I did not see it earlier was always accompanied by a larger and looming question. Why had I not done more to stop it? As much as I would like to deny it, I now understand there is a direct line between the election night I celebrated in 2000 and the night I mourned in 2016.

It is difficult to imagine two more different men than George W. Bush and Donald Trump. Bush's 2000 acceptance speech at the Republican National Convention reads like an artifact from a lost civilization. It's a plea for optimism, hope, and compassion. That candidate has no place in the Republican Party of 2023. But as different as Bush and Trump are, the Supreme Court's role in the 2000 presidential election proved to be a model for the slow-burning legal assault on our democracy that roared to a forest fire when Donald Trump refused to accept the outcome of the 2020 election.

To Trump and his supporters, which included a large majority of the Republican members of the House of Representatives, the 2000 election was a gateway drug to their efforts to steal the 2020 election. Once the outcome of a presidential race is decided in court and not at the ballot box, it's logical to view the legal system as an extension of a campaign, rather than the foundation upon which civil society is built. Donald Trump was not allowed to remain in office, but it would be a grave mistake to think that the efforts of January 6, 2021, failed. The refusal of the Republican Party to acknowledge that he lost a not-very-close presidential race has accelerated America's division into two distinct groups. One side believes that America has a legally elected president, and one does not. If America does slide into autocracy, those two opposing points of view will have proven to be an essential element in the death of democracy. The last time Americans couldn't agree on who was a legal president was in 1861.

————

There is nothing new about a country with stark societal divides. In the mid-nineteenth century, Disraeli wrote a novel with the not very subtle title *Sybil, or The Two Nations*.

In the opening scene, a character describes England as being:

> Two nations; between whom there is no intercourse and no sympathy; who are as ignorant of each other's habits, thoughts, and feelings, as if they were dwellers in different zones, or inhabitants of different planets; who are formed by a different breeding, are fed by a different food, are ordered by different manners, and are not governed by the same laws.
>
> "You speak of—" said Egremont, hesitatingly, *"The Rich and the Poor."*

Disraeli's "two nations" were divided by class and money, the two elements, together with race, that so often segment societies. But in America, while there is tremendous inequality, our greatest political divide is one of choice, not circumstances. Two families living next door to each other with similar incomes can believe they live in starkly different nations. One family believes their government is legal, while the other is utterly convinced it's illegal. The overriding question is a basic one: How long can we survive this?

Two truths remain constant in this moment of American peril. The first is that if there is to be a democracy, someone must be willing to lose. The second is that no one tries to change the rules of a game they are winning.

At the heart of the Republican Party's coordinated, dedicated, and patient efforts to change the legal parameters of how American democracy functions is the deep fear that the party is doomed. The majority of Americans under fifteen are non-white, and the odds are overwhelming that they will remain non-white when they turn eighteen and are eligible to vote. Demographics don't have to be political destiny, but when a party abandons any serious effort to broaden its appeal, the dominance of demographics becomes inevitable.

The demographic apocalypse confronting the Republican Party is both a powerful motivation for it to do whatever it takes to guarantee victory and its justification for doing so. If you believe that America was chosen by God to be a white, Christian nation, then the looming specter of a minority-majority America demands action. The reason so many Republicans have started to label Democrats as "pedophiles" and "groomers" is the same as why the Russians call the Jewish president of Ukraine a "Nazi." Any normal parameters of accepted behavior are upended when the alternative is an existential threat to all that is good and decent.

In the aftermath of January 6, 2021, it's often observed that a coup attempt in which the leaders go unpunished should properly be called practice, not justice. That is both true and misleading. For those who voted *not* to certify the election and refuse to accept that Donald Trump lost a fair election, the goal isn't for the next coup to succeed. Their objective is to make a coup unnecessary. If a state with a Republican legislature passes a law allowing the legislature to overturn the popular vote in a presidential election, when it happens, it isn't a coup. It's perfectly legal.

The difficulty with imagining the unimaginable is that it's truly difficult to imagine. A phrase like "the end of democracy in America" easily calls to mind some violent confrontation with tanks rolling down Pennsylvania Avenue. At a QAnon conference in 2021, Michael Flynn, the former general Trump chose to be his first national security advisor, and who later pled guilty to felony charges of lying to the FBI and was pardoned by Trump, was asked, "I want to know why what happened in Myanmar can't happen here." The crowd cheered, and Flynn answered, "No reason. I mean, it *should* happen here."

But it is unlikely that American democracy ends like Myanmar, with pitched battles in the streets. In a *UCLA Law Review* article, University of Chicago law professors Aziz Huq and Tom Ginsburg describe the two paths leading to autocracy as "authoritarian reversion and constitutional retrogression." They define the differences. "A reversion is a rapid and near-complete collapse of democratic institutions. Retrogression is a more subtle, incremental erosion to three institutional predicates of democracy occurring simultaneously: competitive elections; rights of political speech and association, and the administrative and adjudicative rule of law."

America's slide into autocracy is most likely to follow Hemingway's description of the path to bankruptcy: "gradually and then suddenly." "The process of democratic backsliding in the United States is proceeding in a recognizable way," Amherst political science professor Javier Corrales wrote in the *New York Times*. "Now that the Republican Party has proved that it is unwilling to curb the president's worst impulses, Donald Trump is turning to the next step in his quest for more power for the executive branch, the opposite of what the founders intended with our Constitution." It is chilling that Corrales wrote this in March 2020, forecasting what was to happen post-election.

The Republican authoritarian groundwork was laid by a long-running siege on democracy, utilizing a combination of voter-suppression legislation, gerrymandering, and the elevation of activist judges. This patient strategy is designed to expect and accept some failures for incremental advances. The intent is to layer incremental gain upon incremental gain, slowly normalizing the changes that become the foundation for a self-sustaining autocracy. As Huq and Ginsburg wrote, it is difficult "to observe and evaluate the aggregate effect of many incremental cuts into democratic, liberal, and constitutional norms."

There will never be prime-time nationally televised hearings on laws making it more difficult for students to vote, or on the reduction in voting sites, increased difficulty to register, or the purging of voter rolls. No one dies when these laws are passed. There are no scenes of a mob chanting for the death of a vice president, no Confederate flags paraded through the rotunda of the nation's Capitol. A single suppressive law is never labeled as definitive evidence of the end of democracy, which is exactly the point.

"Autocrats declare their intentions early on," Masha Gessen wrote in *Surviving Autocracy*. "We disbelieve or ignore them at our peril." The grotesque excesses of Donald Trump, his vulgarity and petty feuds, and the celebration of his own ignorance have served him well as an autocratic force. They have allowed the Republican Party and much of what passes for its intellectual cheering squad to focus on the loud and profane while ignoring Trump's constant declarations that he has no use for democracy. "No powerful political actor had set out to destroy the American political system itself, until that is, Trump won the Republican nomination," Gessen writes. "He was probably the first major party nominee who ran not for president but for autocrat. And he won."

It is pathetically absurd when leaders of one of our two major political parties openly wish, "If only he didn't tweet," as a response to the man's intention to destroy democracy. It would be deeply comic were it not so tragic. It has the ring of Monty Python's Black Knight declaring, "'Tis but a scratch," as his limbs are severed.

Before any votes were cast for Trump in the 2016

Republican primary, it was impossible to believe that he had any intention of respecting the U.S. Constitution, a document there is no reason to think he has read. It became necessary for the Republican establishment to develop a framework of denial. It's a construct that Peter Thiel, another billionaire who has openly denounced democracy, articulated perfectly. "The media is always taking Trump literally," Thiel said in an October 2016 speech at the National Press Club. "It never takes him seriously, but it always takes him literally....I think a lot of voters who vote for Trump take Trump seriously but not literally."

Much of the Republican establishment justified supporting Trump by claiming, perhaps even believing, that the institutions of American democracy would serve as a blast wall to protect the country from the destructive force of the man they ushered into the presidency. Today, many would still assert they were proven right. The country survived four years of Trump, even an insurrection, they claim, insisting that we are stronger for the test. It is understandably self-serving when Republicans say it, but it is much more troubling when it comes from those who opposed Trump. Our ability to defend our institutions grows weaker when we assume they are safe, even as the attacks on them grow bolder.

With the Republican Party's help, or its passive silence at best, Trump and Trumpism have attacked the Justice

Department; the FBI; the Bureau of Alcohol, Tobacco, Firearms and Explosives; the seventeen branches of intelligence gathering that agreed Russia helped Trump win; the independence of the military; the integrity of the entire judicial system; the voting process; the counting of votes; the certification of elections; and NATO.

Individual judges and their families have been attacked. Trump attempted to intimidate a judge born in Indiana by calling him a "Mexican" when he was assigned to the case brought against Trump University, only one of the many fraudulent schemes Trump has launched over the years. He has attacked FBI agents and their families, targeting specific poll workers and their families, and harassed secretaries of state and their families, forcing spouses and children to go into hiding for protection.

"Presidents across the world use diverse tactics to achieve unlimited government, but a common approach is to erode the impartiality of the law," Amherst College's Javier Corrales wrote in the *New York Times*. "The goal is always to use and abuse the law to protect yourself and your allies. This is called autocratic legalism."

The 2022 elections were hailed by many as a positive turning point in the battle against Trumpism, but the fact that the election could have been worse does not make it a success. Because of the outcome of that election, Marjorie Taylor Greene is now the second most powerful member of the

House. Given every opportunity to turn away from Trump, Republican elected officials and party leaders overwhelmingly say they will support Trump if he is the 2024 nominee. Even after he was indicted by one New York grand jury and found guilty by another for his sexual abuse and defamation of E. Jean Carroll. He has been indicted on thirty-seven federal charges, and thirty-one counts under the Espionage Act. He faces a very likely indictment for election interference in Georgia. The indictments have solidified Trump's support in the party, and Republican leaders continue to say they will support this potential felon if he is the Republican nominee.

This is where language fails us.

The statement "I will support the nominee of my party" is so benign and boring that it's the political equivalent of "Nice to meet you," a social convention that we don't consider a moral test. Every day, millions of us say this to people we really *aren't* glad to meet, but it doesn't trouble us or make us question our core values. It is just what we say. And so it is with "I will support the nominee of my party." American politicians have been saying this since parties emerged in our political system.

But the context is entirely different when it means supporting a man who succeeded in ending the peaceful transition of power—people died during the Trump insurrection—and was elected with the help of the Russians, who have openly declared they will continue to attack the American electoral system to support him. "We have interfered, we are interfering, and we will continue to interfere," Yevgeny Prigozhin said in March 2023. He's the same Russian who runs the Wagner mercenary group and prides himself on the barbaric execution of enemies by beating their brains out with his trademark sledgehammer or cutting off their heads.

Alarms have been raised about the efforts of Republicans, many of them successful, to use the legal system to influence election outcomes. But often overlooked in the discussions of voter suppression, gerrymandering, and the efforts to control the counting of votes is the recognition that the Republican Party has grown from a center-right democratic institution into an autocratic force.

In some ways, the Republican Party still bears the *appearance* of a normal American party. It hasn't changed its name, members haven't started wearing uniforms, and regular meetings of the party hierarchy continue to be held in fancy resorts around the country. This outward appearance of normalcy is a cloak that hides the radical essence of a party that does not believe America has a legal commander-in-chief. On a fundamental level, its position on democracy is no different from radical 1960s groups like Students for a Democratic Society or the Symbionese Liberation Army, who maintained that the American government was illegitimate. But those groups never had the power to alter the legal structure of a democracy to help them acquire and maintain power. The fact that the Republican Party has offices and organizations in every state, that it has a large headquarters adjacent to the Capitol, and that millions of Americans support Republicans does not normalize the organization. It makes it more dangerous.

There are vastly more supporters of Donald Trump and the Republican Party who are heavily armed and eager to attack the U.S. government than ever belonged to any radical group in American history. The SDS was a handful of radicals; the members of the Symbionese Liberation Army could all ride together in a van. As I detail in the next chapter, "The Shock Troops," the Republican Party benefits from a loose affiliation of violent groups who have proven they will use force to attack the United States government when they are called into action by an autocrat like Donald Trump. In a debate with Joe Biden on September 29, 2020, Trump urged the Proud Boys to "stand back and stand by." On January 6, 2021, he told them their time had come and called them to Washington.

————

The heart of the Big Lie that the 2020 election was stolen is the useful fiction of voter fraud that the Republican Party has been pushing for decades. I worked in Republican campaigns for thirty years, won and lost many close races. Not once did I see any evidence of voter fraud. The problem we have in America is that we can't get people to vote even when it's perfectly legal. Any claims that there are millions of people who are eager to commit a felony by voting has always been ridiculous. The truth is that no one in the Republican Party actually believes there is widespread fraud, but it is a convenient cover story for the incremental destruction of democracy.

The ever-increasing voter-restriction laws that are pushed in Republican legislatures are written under the pretext of the urgent need to solve a problem that does not exist. Their true intent is to lend a veneer of higher purpose to multiple efforts intended to discourage the voters who are least likely to vote Republican from actually voting. On the surface, there is an insidious logic to these efforts. Any law passed will apply to all citizens, the Republicans insist, so how can you claim that one party or group is being unfairly targeted?

In practice, however, the demographic divide between the two parties allows laws to be designed with a disproportionate impact on those who are unlikely to vote Republican. Any law that makes it more difficult to vote favors Republicans; laws that expand the ease of voting help Democrats.

There is a simple formula with which voters can be targeted as likely Democratic or Republican. The higher your income, the more likely you are to vote Republican. The only economic group that Trump won in 2020 was those voters who make over $100,000 a year. As the Pew Research Center reported, "When it comes to choosing a party's candidate in the voting booth, one pattern in modern American politics is so familiar it has become a truism: the rich vote Republican, the poor vote Democratic."

The impact of financial inequality affects every aspect of the electoral process. Those with higher incomes are registered to vote in disproportionate numbers. Over 80 percent of the wealthiest Americans are registered to vote, a percentage that decreases with each drop in income. Only 22 percent of the poorest Americans are registered to vote. Among all those who register and show up to vote, the likelihood that they will vote Republican increases in reverse order from the bottom of the economic ladder to the top.

It's obvious why Republicans have consistently pressed to make it harder to register and more difficult to vote. In 2015, when Donald Trump began openly to challenge the legitimacy of any election he didn't win, he was building on the well-seasoned doubts of election integrity Republicans have used for decades to justify their highly focused efforts to curate the electorate. The "Big Lie" was simply an amplification of the time-tested voter-fraud lie.

Both parties are constantly engaged in efforts to change voting laws. The difference is that Democrats consistently try to broaden voter participation, while Republicans attempt to shrink it. Given their different electoral bases, both are in their party's best interest but both are not in America's best interest. One engages more citizens in the process of democracy and one aims to reduce their involvement. The Brennan Center tracks voting rights–related legislation in every state. Its December 2021 report stated the following:

> Between January 1 and December 7, at least nine-teen states passed thirty-four laws restricting access to voting. More than 440 bills with provisions that restrict voting access have been introduced in forty-nine states in the 2021 legislative sessions. These numbers are extraordinary: state legislatures enacted far more restrictive voting laws in 2021 than in any year since the Brennan Center began tracking voting legislation in 2011. More than a third of all restrictive voting laws enacted since then were passed this year. And in a new trend this year, legislators introduced bills to allow partisan actors to interfere with election processes or even reject election results entirely.

The Brennan Center's 2022 report found that 408 restrictive bills were introduced in thirty-nine states, with eight states passing new voter restrictions. An additional 151 election interference bills were introduced, with seven states passing twelve new laws. The center defines election-interference laws as measures that "allow for partisan interference in the election process, including directing new resources to pursue the prosecution of election officials for ordinary conduct, establishing biased election review processes, or prohibiting the use of machines to count ballots for any election."

In 2023, the pattern has escalated and is on track for a record number of bills to be introduced that are aimed at restricting voting or increasing interference. But as the Brennan Center notes, "This expansive legislation does not balance the scales. The states that have enacted restrictive laws tend to be ones in which voting is already relatively difficult, while the states that have enacted expansive laws tend to have relatively more accessible voting processes."

Compare the two approaches taken by Wisconsin and Florida to deal with restoring voting rights to people who were convicted of felonies. Wisconsin expanded voting rights for the 55,000 former felons who were previously excluded. All who once were denied the right to vote because of their convictions had their rights restored.

Similarly, Floridians passed "Amendment 4" in 2018, amending the state constitution to reinstate voting rights for people with felony convictions who had completed all the terms of their sentence, excluding those convicted of murder or sex offenses. The measure passed overwhelmingly by a margin of 64.5 percent to 35.5 percent. That same year, Florida elected Ron DeSantis governor. He defeated the African American mayor of Tallahassee by the narrowest margin in modern Florida gubernatorial history, a little more than 30,000 votes out of 8 million votes cast.

With the passage of Amendment 4, an estimated 1.4 million more Floridians were now eligible to vote. In a state with a history of close elections, the expanded voter pool had the potential to alter the electoral landscape for years. More than one in five of these reinstated voters were Black. As former felons began to register, they began to declare themselves Democrats twice as often as Republicans.

For a governor who had won an election by only 30,000 votes, the passage of Amendment 4 was an obvious and serious threat. But there was nothing Florida Republicans could do to change the passage of the new constitutional amendment. Instead, they passed a measure that Governor DeSantis signed into law requiring that "people with felony records pay 'all fines and fees' associated with their sentence prior to the restoration of their voting rights."

It was exactly the sort of tactic that white Southerners had used for decades to limit the impact of laws passed to enfranchise Blacks. A group of former felons sued, arguing that the measure was a poll tax in everything but name, and pointing out that everyday Floridians who owe back taxes or other fines to the state are not disqualified from voting. U.S. District Judge Robert Hinkle agreed and ruled that the new law created an illegal "pay-to-vote" system. His ruling was subsequently over-turned by the U.S. Court of Appeals for the 11th Circuit, five of whose twelve judges were appointed by Donald Trump.

The Florida Rights Restoration Coalition, the group behind the voter initiative, immediately started raising funds to pay any fines or fees of the newly enfranchised for-mer felons. Former New York City Mayor Michael Bloom-berg donated $16 million, and Michael Jordan and LeBron James pledged millions more. A University of Florida politi-cal science professor estimated that 775,000 former felons had outstanding fines that totaled almost $1 billion.

But even those felons who had the resources to pay their fines found it almost impossible to find out how much they owed. No central database could determine how much, if anything, any individual owed. It was a classic case of Catch-22, and it had the intended effect of all but reversing the constitutional amendment that had been overwhelm-ingly passed by Florida voters.

In April 2022, Governor DeSantis announced with great fanfare the creation of a new Office of Election Crimes and Security in the Florida Department of State to review fraud allegations and conduct investigations. This created, in effect, a voter-fraud police force whose members would be appointed by DeSantis. The governor implemented this new "election crimes" unit despite the fact that he had praised the very successful 2020 Florida election, one in which his state "was able to handle 11 million ballots, a combination of in-person early voting, vote-by-mail, Election Day, process them in a timely way, tabulate them, and report them."

So, given that admittedly smooth election, why did DeSantis now believe that voter fraud was suddenly such a critical problem that he created the only voter-fraud police force in America at a cost of over $1 million? What followed made it obvious. In a state of over 22 million people, the DeSantis-appointed cops arrested precisely twenty people for alleged voter fraud, all of them former felons who had voted. They were charged with not having paid their outstanding fines and fees before voting. Of those twenty, two pled guilty. Ron DeSantis wasted over $1 million of taxpayers' money to fund a personal police force to prove to Republican primary voters that he was willing to use the power of the state to intimidate non-Republican voters.

Like all extremist movements, the GOP is now caught up in a cycle of purity tests across the country, where competition for leadership is determined by a willingness to be the most extreme, and it's a cycle that will continue until there is an intervening force. There was a time when it would have been reasonable to hope, if not assume, that restraint would come from within the party. But at every opportunity the party has to veer back to a traditional model of a political party in a democracy, it accelerates in the opposite direction toward autocracy.

Blatant power grabs like DeSantis's in Florida are increasingly defended by the assertion that America was intended to be a constitutional republic, not a democracy. It's a claim that is both true and terribly misleading. America was founded by people who deeply distrusted a powerful central government and assumed that decisions were best made by "leaders," who were assumed to be educated white men who owned property. *The Federalist Papers* of Alexander Hamilton and James Madison considered this such an essential point that it was printed in full caps in Federalist No. 63. The two men believed "IN THE TOTAL EXCLUSION OF THE PEOPLE, IN THEIR COLLECTIVE CAPACITY, from any share" in governing. Their vision was that public policy should be made by elected representatives "whose wisdom may best discern the true interest of their country."

This is the constitutional theory embraced by Republicans like Utah Senator Mike Lee, who tweeted in outrage in the middle of the Pence-Harris vice-presidential debate, "We are not a democracy!" There is something deeply ironic about Republicans who support a man who attempted to end the American Experiment by claiming to represent the true values of those who created the American Experiment. But their rejection of democracy as original intent also relies on a narrow and limited interpretation, ignoring the fact that two and a half centuries ago it was a very different world. In an article published in *The Atlantic* immediately prior to the 2020 election titled "'America Is a Republic, Not a Democracy' Is a Dangerous—and Wrong—Argument," political science professor George Thomas of Claremont McKenna College wrote:

> When founding thinkers such as James Madison spoke of democracy, they were usually referring to *direct* democracy, what Madison frequently labeled "pure" democracy. Madison made the distinction between a republic and a direct democracy exquisitely clear in "Federalist No. 14: In a democracy, the people meet and exercise the government in person; in a republic, they assemble and administer it by their representatives and agents. A democracy, consequently, will be confined to a small spot. A republic may be extended over a large region." Both a democracy and a republic were *popular* forms of government: Each drew its legitimacy from the people and depended on rule by the people. The crucial difference was that a republic relied on representation, while in a "pure" democracy, the people represented themselves.

Senator Lee and others who rely on the "republic not a democracy" justification for ignoring the majority will can't come out and say what they clearly would prefer: America would be better off if we went back to the original concept of the Founding Fathers and only allowed white men who owned property to vote.

The demographic changes in America are devastating for the electoral future of the Republican Party. But the geographic distribution of the changing demographics, combined with the Constitution's establishment of the U.S. Senate and the electoral college, have increasingly enabled a minority of the country to override the views and votes of the majority.

For most of my political life, I didn't spend much time thinking about what our political system would be like without the electoral college. It seemed a waste of time, like pondering the possibility of a world in which gravity was a regional phenomenon. After the 2000 Bush campaign, some of us joked that anybody could win a presidential race simply by getting more votes, but it takes professionals if you lose by half a million. It seemed more amusing then.

In 2000, it had been over a hundred years since the winner of the popular vote did not win the presidency, and there was no reason to believe that it wouldn't be another century before it happened again. But then Trump won in 2016, and if 44,000 or so votes in exactly the right places had switched in 2020, he would have won again, despite losing the popular election by over 7 million votes.

Because of the electoral college, the most radical

president in U.S. history was elected by a minority of the voters. The likelihood of this becoming the norm is growing, and it is reflective of larger factors that have given us a Supreme Court majority confirmed by senators who represent a minority of voters, three of whom were appointed by a president who lost the popular vote. It's fair to consider that those three justices are actually five. Two others, Justices John Roberts and Samuel Alito, were appointed by George W. Bush in his second term. He won that term with a majority of the popular vote, but as someone who worked in both Bush campaigns, odds are slim that he would have been elected in 2004 if he had not won in 2000 while losing the popular vote.

The shift in population has transformed the Senate into a legislative body elected by an increasing minority of Americans. While the Senate remains composed of two senators from each state, big states are growing much faster than smaller states. Virginia was the largest state in 1790 with a population thirteen times that of Delaware, the smallest. California now has sixty-eight times as many residents as Wyoming. Twelve percent of the American population lives in California, but just 0.17 percent lives in Wyoming. Republican senators last represented a majority of the U.S. population in 1996, yet they controlled the Senate from 1995 through 2007 and again from 2015 until 2021. Over 40 million more Americans voted for Democratic senators than Republican senators when the Republican Party last controlled the Senate.

We live in a country in which the current U.S. Senate was elected by a minority of American voters. Of the 116 Supreme Court Justices in our country's history, only five have been confirmed by senators representing a minority of the population. All five are on the Court today. This toxic combination is how a minority asserts its views on critical issues like abortion and gun control. "We are far and away the most counter-majoritarian democracy in the world," Steven Levitsky, a professor of government at Harvard University and a coauthor of the book *How Democracies Die*, told David Leonhardt of the *New York Times*.

The success Republicans have had gerrymandering congressional districts is a supercharged propellant for minority rule. But it wasn't always like this. In 1989, President George H. W. Bush proposed a federal ban on gerrymandering. In the *Washington Post*, reporter Ann Devroy wrote that Bush's plan "includes legislation that would create what the White House calls 'neutral criteria' to be used in drawing the nation's congressional districts after the 1990 census."

This was at a time when Democrats had controlled Congress since 1957, so Bush's motivation was not purely good government. It was designed to blunt Democratic advantages following the 1990 census. Over the next two years, Republicans introduced three different voting reform bills to eliminate gerrymandering. But in a reversal of what happened to voting reform legislation after the 2020 election, no Democrat supported the ban.

Twenty years after that census, and following the disastrous 2010 midterm election for Democrats, the Republican Party launched an initiative focused on redistricting following the 2010 census. Called REDMAP—for Redistricting Majority Project—the plan targeted statehouses in which flipping a few seats from Democratic to Republican would shift the balance to Republican control. Months before the 2010 election, Republican political consultant Karl Rove wrote a piece for the *Wall Street Journal* laying out the opportunity for Republicans. "The political world is fixated on whether this year's elections will deliver an epic rebuke of President Barack Obama and his party. If that happens, it could end up costing Democrats congressional seats for a decade to come." He was right.

Rove got his start in politics working for George H. W. Bush and went on to become George W. Bush's chief strategist and the architect of both Bush White House victories. I worked closely with Karl in those elections, and I have no hesitation whatsoever in calling him a genius. More than anyone I worked with in politics, Rove had the ability to see both the near-term tactical demands of politics and the long-term strategic goals. When Rove speculated on the potential for Republicans in 2010, he did so less than eighteen months after Obama's sweeping victory in states John Kerry had lost four years earlier. In the South, Obama won North Carolina and Virginia. He won the 2004 Bush states of Florida, Ohio, Colorado, and Nevada. He even won Dan Quayle's home state of Indiana.

The consensus was that 2008 was a transformative election. But over the Obama years, Democrats lost over nine hundred state-legislature seats, twelve governorships, sixty-nine House seats, and thirteen Senate seats. Some of this could be explained by the difficulty a party in power normally has in holding on to seats in midterm elections, but this trend was maximized by the efforts of REDMAP. Elizabeth Kolbert described the results in *The New Yorker*. "The wins were sufficient to push twenty chambers from a Democratic to a Republican majority. Most significantly, they gave the GOP control over both houses of the legislature in twenty-five states.... The blue map was now red." In 2021, the Associated Press analyzed what had occurred and concluded, "Republican politicians used census data to draw voting districts that gave them a greater political advantage in more states than either party had in the past fifty years."

In his book *RatF**ked*, which details what the Republicans achieved with REDMAP, David Daley sums it up: "It's legal, it's breathtaking, and much of it happened in plain sight. The Democratic majority was ratfucked."

People in the armed forces are fond of the term "combined arms maneuver." The U.S. Army's *Military Review* defines it as "the application of the elements of combat power in a complementary and reinforcing manner to achieve physical, temporal, or psychological advantages over the enemy to preserve freedom of action and exploit success." This is exactly how Republican efforts to shape elections should be perceived. The Republicans have successfully undertaken "complementary and reinforcing" efforts to control legislatures and appoint conservative judges at every level for decades.

A gathering at Yale University on the last weekend in April 1982 turned out to be the "Patient Zero" of the conservative plan to transform the American judiciary. The meeting's title was hardly incendiary—"A Symposium on Federalism: Legal and Political Ramifications"—but out of this single conference grew a network of well-funded groups that ultimately achieved extraordinary impact. Ted Olson, who was then an assistant attorney general in the Department of Justice, said in a weekend talk, "I sense that we are at one of those points in history where the pendulum may be beginning to swing in another direction." Olson would go on to argue successfully for the Republicans in *Bush v. Gore* and be appointed solicitor general by Bush. Tragically, his wife, Barbara Olson, a conservative lawyer and television commentator, was aboard the airliner that crashed into the Pentagon on September 11, 2001.

It's impossible to overstate the impact of what began that weekend in New Haven, Connecticut, and ultimately became the "Federalist Society." The six currently serving Supreme Court justices who were appointed by a Republican president were all members of the Federalist Society. Ninety percent of all the judicial appointments made by Donald Trump were members. When he ran for president in 2016, Donald Trump referenced the Federalist Society to help reassure conservatives who might otherwise have had doubts about a man who had spent most of his life as a pro-choice Democrat, donating to hated Democratic figures such as Chuck Schumer and Anthony Weiner. Trump promised that his judicial nominees would "all [be] picked by the Federalist Society," and he released a list of twenty-one possible Supreme Court justices, all of whom came from their ranks.

The Federalist Society attempts to be seen as a legal organization that vets and recommends judges—much like a conservative version of the American Bar Association. "I have a very simple rule, which is, I'm engaged in the battle of ideas, and I care very deeply about our Constitution and the role of courts in our society," Leonard Leo, who has headed the group since its founding, told the *Washington Post*. "And

I don't waste my time on stories that involve money and politics because what I care about is ideas."

People who believe that also think Jeff Bezos is just a guy who runs a bookstore. Justice Clarence Thomas called Leo "the number three most powerful person in the world" at a Federalist Society meeting in 2018. Although the crowd laughed and Leo responded, "God help us," there is no one else in America running a legal organization that Supreme Court justices joke about running the world.

With the Federalist Society as his base, he has built what the *New York Times* calls "an opaque, sprawling network shaped by Mr. Leo and funded by wealthy patrons." In 2005, Leo formed the Judicial Confirmation Network, raising $15 million to help secure Senate and public support for George W. Bush's Supreme Court nominees John Roberts and Samuel Alito. Since that time, Leo has continued to build out a network of interconnected groups to push conservative judges at the federal and state level. The *Washington Post* reported that "between 2014 and 2017 alone, [the Federalist Society] collected more than $250 million in donations, sometimes known as 'dark money.'" Although each was a separate legal entity, "The groups in Leo's network often work in concert and are linked to Leo and one another by finances, shared board members, phone numbers, addresses, back-office support, and other operational details, according to tax filings, incorporation records, other documents, and interviews."

In August 2022, the *Times* broke a story that a relatively unknown billionaire named Barre Seid had donated 100 percent of the shares of an electronics manufacturing company based in Chicago to a nonprofit controlled by Leo called the Marble Freedom Trust. It then sold the company to an Irish conglomerate for $1.6 billion, an arrangement that shielded the transaction from taxes. This was the largest single donation ever given to a political organization.

Marble Freedom Trust is organized as a private trust, not a corporation, so it has no requirement to publicly disclose any information about its operation. It was formed in Utah and lists its address as a North Salt Lake house that is owned by a former clerk for Justice Clarence Thomas. The group's name does not appear in any public database of business, tax, or securities records. A recent North Carolina Supreme Court ruling is a perfect example of the cumulative impact of decades of work by Republicans to ensure that their party's candidates always win. On April 28, 2023, the North Carolina Supreme Court overturned a previous ruling that partisan gerrymandering was illegal. It's a state that has been a presidential battleground for a long time. North Carolina was won by Obama in 2008, Romney in 2012, and Trump in 2016 and 2020, the 2020 margin just a single digit. It has a Democratic governor, secretary of state, and attorney general. The state Senate and House are both held by Republicans, and thanks to one House member switching from the Democratic to the Republican Party following the 2022 election, Republicans have a supermajority that is veto-proof.

"The ruling clears the way for North Carolina legislators to aggressively gerrymander the congressional map, which is currently represented by seven Democrats and seven Republicans," *Politico* reported. "Now Republicans in Raleigh could re-create the map they initially passed last cycle, which a Democratic-controlled state Supreme Court struck down, netting as many as four seats."

North Carolina once had been a model for nonpartisan judicial elections in the United States. In 2002, the Democratically controlled North Carolina legislature passed a public financing law for the state's judicial races. It was an effort to clean up judicial elections, allowing candidates the choice of entering a public-financing system that provided an equal amount of funding to judicial candidates if they agreed to limit their spending. Over the next ten years, 80 percent of the candidates opted into the public financing system.

But then, the 2010 *Citizens United* Supreme Court decision allowed undisclosed groups to spend unlimited money on campaigns. In the 2012 North Carolina Supreme Court race, an outside group played a major role in running a vicious and largely false negative campaign in support of the Republican-supported conservative candidate. As James

Piltch described it in *The Atlantic*, the "ad in the Newby-Ervin race augured a fundamental change in the politics of North Carolina's judiciary.... North Carolina had tried to take the judiciary out of politics—and politics out of the judiciary—but its reforms were no match for the flood of money in politics following *Citizens United* and Republican efforts to take over the courts after the Tea Party wave."

With Republicans in control of the state legislature, they were successful in killing the judicial-funding system following the 2012 election. Paul Newby, the conservative judge supported by the outside group's negative campaign, won and is now the chief justice of the North Carolina Supreme Court that ruled in favor of partisan gerrymandering.

Any hope that even the most unreasonable state gerrymandering could be appealed to the U.S. Supreme Court ended in 2019 when the Court ruled on a North Carolina case, *Rucho v. Common Cause*. In that litigation, Common Cause appealed a decision that allowed Republicans to follow a plan that was described by Republican Representative David Lewis, chairman of the Redistricting Committee, as "draw[ing] the maps to give a partisan advantage to ten Republicans and three Democrats because I do not believe it's possible to draw a map with eleven Republicans and two Democrats." This is in a state with an equal number of registered Republicans and Democrats.

In 2013, the U.S. Supreme Court gutted the Voting

Rights Act by nullifying Section 5, an existing law that Chief Justice John Roberts had opposed for decades. When he was just twenty-six, Roberts had worked as an aide to Attorney General William French Smith, following a clerkship with Justice William Rehnquist, who at the time was the most conservative judge to serve on the Supreme Court in decades. This was 1981, and Congress was facing a vote to reauthorize the Voting Rights Act. Roberts thought this was a horrendous mistake and wrote to his boss, "Something must be done to educate the senators on the seriousness of this problem." After the reauthorization passed the House and was headed to the Senate, he wrote that the law was "not only constitutionally suspect but also contrary to the most fundamental tenants [*sic*] of the legislative process on which the laws of this country are based."

Taken individually, none of these judicial actions is a death blow to democracy, but collectively, each builds on the previous one. It is a long game played with patience. A timeline tells the story:

1982: The Federalist Society is formed.
1986: Federalist Society superstar Antonin Scalia is nominated to the U.S. Supreme Court by President Reagan.
1991: Clarence Thomas, a Federalist Society member, is nominated by George H. W. Bush.

2000: George W. Bush loses the popular vote to Al Gore but is elected by the electoral college. The Supreme Court rules 5–4 in favor of Bush in the *Bush v. Gore* case.

2004: George W. Bush is reelected.

2005: Leonard Leo of the Federalist Society creates the Judicial Confirmation Network (later to become Judicial Crisis Network). He raises $15 million from undisclosed donors to run confirmation campaigns supporting Bush Supreme Court nominees.

2005: John Roberts, a Federalist Society member, is nominated to the Supreme Court by George W. Bush.

2005: Samuel Alito, a Federalist Society member, is nominated to the Supreme Court by George W. Bush.

2006: The Federalist Society expands its public relations campaign. Leo comments that "I spend probably close to $800,000 annually on a PR team at the Federalist Society, and we generate press that has a publicity value of approximately $146 million each year."

2010: The Supreme Court rules 5–4 in the *Citizens United* decision that corporations have the right to spend unlimited money in U.S. elections. Four of the five deciding votes are cast by Federalist Society members.

2010: REDMAP is formed by Republicans to focus on redistricting state legislatures to maximize Republican benefit.

2012: With the help of undisclosed "dark" money made possible by *Citizens United*, conservative Paul Newby is elected to the North Carolina Supreme Court.

2012: North Carolina ends public financing of judicial nominations.

2013: The Supreme Court nullifies key provisions of the Voting Rights Act, which John Roberts first opposed in 1981.

2016: Justice Scalia dies seven months before the presidential election. Senate Majority Leader Mitch McConnell refuses to allow hearings or a vote on President Obama's choice of Merrick Garland as Scalia's replacement. McConnell says, "The American people should have a voice in the selection of their next Supreme Court justice. Therefore, this vacancy should not be filled until we have a new president."

2016: Leonard Leo's Judicial Crisis Network spends $7 million to support the Republican senators running for reelection who refuse to hold hearings on Merrick Garland.

2016–2017: Groups controlled by Leonard Leo raise over $250 million from undisclosed donors.

2016: Donald Trump loses the popular vote to Hillary Clinton by 2.8 million voters but wins the electoral college.

2017: Trump nominates Neil Gorsuch, a Federalist Society member, to replace Justice Scalia.

2017: Leonard Leo's Judicial Crisis Network spends $10 million supporting the Gorsuch nomination.

2018: Justice Kennedy resigns. Trump appoints Brett Kavanaugh to replace him. Kavanaugh, a Federalist Society member, worked for the two George W. Bush campaigns and in the White House, married Bush's long-time personal assistant, and was nominated by Bush to the United States Court of Appeals for the District of Columbia Circuit. Trump, a president who lost the popular vote, appoints the protégé of a president—Bush—who also lost the popular vote.

2018: The Leonard Leo organization "Freedom and Opportunity Group" donates $4 million to "Independent Women's Voice," which runs ads supporting Kavanaugh. Heather Higgins, the group's president and chief executive, attacks the women who accuse Kavanaugh of sexual assault, saying, "If you have a weak standard of evidence, then what you are doing is guaranteeing that future nominations will all be last-minute character assassinations and circuses." She is paid $311,000 annually as the leader of Independent Women's Voice.

2019: The U.S. Supreme Court rules that states are free to gerrymander without review by the state's Supreme Court. "We conclude that partisan gerrymandering claims present political questions beyond the reach of the federal courts." Of the justices voting in support of the 5–4 ruling, three have been confirmed by a collection of senators who represented a minority of the country's population. All are Federalist Society members.

2020: Justice Ruth Bader Ginsburg dies thirty-eight days before the presidential election. Trump appoints Amy Coney Barrett to replace her. Majority Leader McConnell holds hearings and the Senate vote to confirm her *after* the presidential election voting has begun in many states. He denies this contradicts his previous refusal to hold hearings

on the Merrick Garland nomination during an
election year.

2020: Barrett is confirmed and becomes a justice of
the Supreme Court. There have been five Supreme
Court justices in U.S. history who were appointed
by a president elected with a minority of the vote
and confirmed by senators representing a minority
of the country's population. With Barrett's
confirmation, all five are currently on the Supreme
Court.

2022: $1.6 billion is gifted to the Marble Freedom
Trust, a Leonard Leo group.

2023: The North Carolina Supreme Court overturns
a previous ruling and allows the Republican-
controlled legislature to draw districts by any
guidelines they choose. The 2019 Supreme Court
ruling on gerrymandering provides no pathway for
appeal. Justice Paul Newby, who was elected post–
Citizens United, is now chief justice.

What began decades earlier continues to play out,
changing the legal basis of American elections. It is a long
game played patiently and relentlessly with no like effort in
opposition.

———

The Republican attack on the electoral system with combined efforts to challenge election results, restrict voting, and control the counting of votes is following the successful blueprint used by the Federalist Society to change the judicial system. Leonard Leo has formed a group called the Honest Elections Project that is pushing the "independent state legislature theory" that would give "state legislatures exclusive and near-absolute power to regulate federal elections," the Brennan Center wrote in a 2022 study. "The result? When it comes to federal elections, legislators would be free to violate the state constitution, and state courts couldn't stop them."

The theory hinges on interpretation of the specific language in Article I, Section 4 of the U.S. Constitution: "The Times, Places and Manner of holding Elections for Senators and Representatives, shall be prescribed in each State by the Legislature thereof." The Court heard oral arguments in December 2022 in *Moore v. Harper*, a North Carolina gerrymandering case that became the first test of the theory.

On June 27, 2023, the Court ruled 6–3 that the Elections Clause does not give state legislatures full control of federal elections. The decision was rightfully celebrated as a victory for democracy, but there are now three Supreme Court judges who have voiced support for what amounts to the end of American democracy as it has existed. Using the

Federalist Society's long-game model, this is incremental progress upon which future victories will be built.

In Mark Meadows's last days as Trump's fourth White House chief of staff, he was texting Ginni Thomas, Justice Clarence Thomas's wife, his reassurance that God was on the side of those trying to overthrow the government of the United States. "This is a fight of good versus evil," Meadows wrote. "Evil always looks like the victor until the King of Kings triumphs. Do not grow weary in well doing. The fight continues. I have staked my career on it." In the January 6th congressional investigation, Ginni Thomas emerged as a wacky, insurrectionist-loving Lady Macbeth figure. If it is discovered that she has been burying bodies in her backyard for years, her texts to Meadows will serve her well in a future insanity plea. "Biden crime family & ballot fraud co-conspirators (elected officials, bureaucrats, social media censorship mongers, fake stream media reporters, etc) are being arrested & detained for ballot fraud right now & over coming days, & will be living in barges off GITMO to face military tribunals for sedition."

Meadows is now a top advisor to the Conservative Partnership Institute, a typically bland name for an organization dedicated to accomplishing the goals of the January 6 insurrection. With a budget of over $45 million, it acts as a hub for election deniers, including Cleta Mitchell, who serves as a "Senior Legal Fellow." Mitchell joins a long list of those who had perfectly normal careers before eagerly buying a ticket on the Trump crazy train. Mitchell was once the force behind Oklahoma's passage of the Equal Rights Amendment as a Democratic member of the Oklahoma legislature. She became involved in the term limits movement in the 1990s and drifted rightward. When Trump was elected, she was a partner in the DC law firm of Foley and Lardner, which is as establishment Washington as it gets. Then, on January 2, 2021, she was in the Oval Office when Trump called the Georgia Secretary of State and pressured him to do what was necessary to reverse the election results. "All I want to do is this. I just want to find 11,780 votes, which is one more than we have because we won the state."

Over the course of the call, Mitchell repeatedly interjected to push the Georgia Secretary of State Brad Raffensperger and his lawyers, attempting to bring some coherence to the jumbled confusion of contradictory numbers and conspiracy theories that Trump was regurgitating. At one point they had this exchange:

> *Trump:* No, but I told you. We're not, we're not saying that.
> *Mitchell:* We did say that.

Mitchell's law firm had asserted that it was not involved in any election denial efforts. When the *Washington Post* broke the story of the call, Mitchell's defense was that she was not Trump's attorney of record. But once you're sitting in the Oval Office helping a president pressure an election official to reverse the outcome of a presidential election, that's a nuance of little meaning. She resigned from her firm and now is part of the broad Republican effort to elect election officials who embrace the Big Lie. Why try to convince an honorable election official when you can elect one who is on your side? Much more efficient.

In low-profile events that are largely hidden from the press, a coalition of Republican groups that call themselves the "Election Integrity Network" hold regular meetings for election officials, their staffs, and potential poll workers as part of a multipronged strategy to change the electoral process in America. "This fight is not just about what happened in 2020," Mark Meadows said two years after his involvement in the failed Trump coup. "This fight is about every future election, whether it is at a state level or a federal level or the highest office in the land."

At one meeting in Arizona in the spring of 2022, leaked audio revealed Cleta Mitchell expanding on the Great Replacement Theory of a Democratic plot to reduce the power of white voters. She showed a picture of Jesse Jackson speaking at the Pepsi-sponsored Goodwill Games between the United States and the Soviet Union in front of the flags of both nations. "You know the American flag. Do you know what that other flag is?" Mitchell asked, pointing to the Soviet flag. "The Communist Party of America. This was the 1980s. And Pepsi—you think that this is new? This business of the woke corporations throwing in with the left? This started a long time ago."

She continued, articulating the fear that unites white movements, from the KKK to the MAGA Republican Party. "That is their goal. If we can mobilize people of color and get them registered to vote we will change America. They call it the 'New American Majority.'"

In another leaked audio tape of Mitchell speaking at an RNC donor meeting, she put it bluntly: "Whenever anybody starts telling you that they're worried about our democracy or protecting our democracy, or they've got a democracy in their name, those are not friends of ours."

One of the great benefits and pleasures of a democracy is not having to think about democracy. In a functioning democratic civil society, the rights and privileges of citizenship should be assumed. The freedom not to be concerned about the mood of an autocrat or the danger of an encroaching state is a great gift of democracy. But today in America, there are people who wake up every day with the intent to end the American Experiment. They are smart, organized, well funded, and powered by the conviction that they are saving the true America. Their mission is evil, but they do not appear evil. These are not brownshirts or drunken brawlers. They are lawyers, politicians, and business leaders. Their blandness is a camouflage for the radical nature of their intent. They believe their victory is inevitable.

As long as those who treasure democracy do not rise to the defense of democracy, the question is not if American democracy will be lost but when. In a country built on the myth of manifest destiny, we must embrace that there is no American destiny. Our greatest mistake would be to believe that America will default to democracy. There will be no dramatic calling of arms to defend a democratic vision of America. Each of us must be our own Paul Revere. Each of us must decide the threat is real and find the battlefield of our choosing.

Autocrats win when they master the freedoms of a democratic society to kill democracy. That is the path we are on today. Where that path leads is up to each of us.

Chapter 5

The Shock Troops

Democracy is a system in which parties lose elections.

—*Adam Przeworski*, Democracy and
the Market *(1991)*

A head of state elected with the help of a hostile foreign power refuses to recognize a crushing defeat. He replaces the country's top law enforcement official with a loyalist. One of the country's highest-ranking retired generals plans to seize ballot boxes and declare martial law. His brother is high in the command structure of the national military. Top aides to the head of state work closely with powerful elected officials in the party to invalidate the elections.

Militia groups that have been training for years are activated and summoned to the nation's capital. Wealthy supporters provide funding for the militias. The party's organization of top law enforcement officials around the country coordinates funding and support for the militias. A legal team for the head of state works closely with the government's top law enforcement attorneys constructing a legal framework for the head of state to remain in power.

On the key day of election certification, the militia groups storm the Capitol attempting to assassinate key members of the government, including those party officials disloyal to the head of state. The brother of the retired general plotting martial law delays additional armed response, allowing the militia to seize most of the Capitol complex. The Capitol guards oppose the coup and engage the militias in an hours-long battle. They suffer over a hundred casualties, the most of any domestic law enforcement officers in a single day in the nation's long history. Finally, with the help of a military not loyal to the head of state, the Capitol is retaken, and the coup fails.

The head of state refuses to acknowledge his defeat, retreating to a private compound in a state with a loyal governor he helped elect. In subsequent years, some members of the militia who stormed the Capitol are convicted of crimes. None of the top planners of the coup, including the head of state and the government officials who supported the coup, are held responsible. Those in the party who opposed the coup are ejected from the party.

The now-former head of state, whose supporters consider him the legal president, plans his campaign to return to the office, promising to pardon any of the convicted militia members. He opens his rallies with a pledge of allegiance to the militia who stormed the Capitol. Across the nation, his party's elected officials work frantically to change election laws to block those opposed to the party from voting. The majority of the party still believes he won the election and that they have a moral obligation to depose the current illegal head of state. The sale of military-grade weapons increases as the next election draws closer.

In the long-ago misty history of this nation—say, ten years ago—such a scenario would have been unimaginable in the United States, possible only in one of those "shithole" countries Donald Trump loves to mock. But it is precisely what happened in our 2020 elections. On one level, it was all very predictable. No one ever expected Donald Trump to behave like a decent human being who respected his country. But the specifics of how it unfolded, no one could have predicted.

And that's the lesson for the future. Those who look to the failure of efforts in 2020 to end the American Experiment as proof are as naïve as those of us—and that was most of us—who would not have predicted Donald Trump would instigate this nation's most successful terrorist attack on our Capitol. There is no need to speculate about who might be drawn to a violent effort to overthrow the United States government. All we need do is look at the January 6 insurrections.

A year after the attack on the Capitol, University of Chicago political scientist Robert Pape published a report titled "American Face of Insurrection: Analysis of Individuals Charged for Storming the US Capitol." He focused on the 716 individuals charged with illegally entering the Capitol as of January 1, 2022. "Our analysis is grounded in detailed data," Pape wrote. His team "systematically identified and collected a broad spectrum of demographic and socioeconomic characteristics as well as militant group ties, and military experience."

The study is a fascinating and often surprising examination of those who were drawn to their nation's capital on January 6. "Those who stormed the Capitol represent a mainstream political movement and are not simply confined to the fringes of American society," the report concluded. "Overall, our analysis shows that we are dealing with a new kind of a right-wing movement, one that is demographically closer to an average American than an average right-wing extremist and indicating that far-right support for political violence is moving into the mainstream."

Forty-three percent of the January 6 insurrectionists were white-collar workers such as business owners, architects, doctors, and lawyers. Pape, who has decades of experience studying global political violence, says this statistic was unexpected. Out of the hundreds of people arrested for breaking into the Capitol, he says only 7 percent were unemployed at the time—nearly the national unemployment average. "Usually, we think we'll get them a job. Well, we've already got over half business owners, CEOs, and folks from white-collar occupations—that's not going to work."

Normally, 40 percent of right-wing extremists have prior military service, whereas January 6 Capitol rioters were about 15 percent, he says. Pape also investigated the rioters' criminal backgrounds and found "30 percent of those who broke into the Capitol on Jan. 6 have a criminal history of some kind, often basically being arrested for drug misdemeanors," he says. "But that compares to 64 percent of right-wing extremists."

Typically, right-wing extremists are young—normally under the age of thirty-four. On January 6, rioters were mostly in their forties and fifties. "This is uncomfortable for a variety of reasons. It means a lot of our usual counter-violent extremist solutions just don't apply," Pape says. Right-wing extremist violence is usually strongly linked to skinhead gangs or militia groups. But 87 percent of the Capitol rioters were not members of violent groups such as the Oath Keepers or Proud Boys. "Far fewer insurrectionists belonged to militias when compared to Right-wing extremist arrests between 2015-2020," the University of Chicago report discovered. "Forty-eight percent of right-wing extremist arrests between 2015-2020 belonged to a militia or group, while only 13 percent of insurrectionists in 2021 belonged to a militia or group."

After January 6, many people assumed the insurrectionists came from deep red parts of the country. But Pape says more than half of those arrested lived in counties that Biden won. Rioters came from America's largest cities and their surrounding suburbs.

Extremists are thought to be on the margins of society—but that's not the case with the Capitol insurrectionists, a mob so massive they were able to overrun the Capitol Police. "What we're seeing is the mainstream married with parts of the fringe, to be sure. I'm not saying the fringe didn't show up at all," he says. "But what made the storm a storm on Jan. 6 was not the fringe participation, but the mainstream."

In one key area, the insurrectionists do match the profile of right-wing extremists. They are overwhelmingly white males. Ninety-three percent of those insurrectionists charged with crimes were white, and 85 percent were male. This matches the demographic of those arrested for crimes associated with right-wing movements in the five years before the insurrection.

And though the majority came from counties that Biden carried, areas that had a declining white population were more likely to produce insurrectionists. The report describes them as areas "where racial and ethnic demographics are actively changing." The more a county supported Trump, the less likely it was to be the home of someone arrested for attacking the Capitol.

In a related article for *The Atlantic*, Pape came to some basic conclusions: "What's clear is that the Capitol riot revealed a new force in American politics—not merely a mix of right-wing organizations, but a broader mass political movement that has violence at its core and draws strength even from places where Trump supporters are in the minority." He cautions against assuming that those drawn to the insurrection will perform like previous groups of right-wing extremists:

Americans who believe in democratic norms should be wary of pat solutions. Some of the standard methods of countering violent extremism—such as promoting employment or waiting patiently for participants to mellow with age—probably won't mollify middle-aged, middle-class insurrectionists. And simply targeting better-established far-right organizations will not prevent people like the Capitol rioters from trying to exercise power by force.

In retrospect, what may be most shocking about the January 6, 2021, attack on the Capitol was that it was shocking. In his classic 1991 study of democracy, *Democracy and the Market: Political and Economic Reforms in Eastern Europe and Latin America*, the Polish-born political scientist Adam Przeworski made a fundamental observation that goes to the heart of the current American crisis. "Democracy is a system in which parties lose elections." Przeworski examines a basic question: In a system that is designed to produce winners and losers, why should those who lose accept defeat? His conclusion: "Political forces comply with present defeats because they believe that the institutional framework that organizes the democratic competition will permit them to advance their interests in the future." It requires an ability to focus beyond an election defeat with faith in the institutions. The belief in those building blocks of democracy allows them "to think about the future rather than being concerned exclusively with present outcomes."

The Trump loyalists who stormed the Capitol have broken faith with the institutions of American democracy. They have stepped out of the American mainstream, and as the government prosecutes January 6 insurrectionists, it is only more proof of the need to fight the power of the Deep State.

For decades, elements of the far right have demonstrated their lack of faith in the governance of the United States by attempting to create their own separate societies. Like all the greatest divides in American history, it was a movement driven by race. After World War II, a member of the California Ku Klux Klan named Wesley Swift founded the Church of Jesus Christ—Christian, a white supremacist cult that called itself a religion. Swift was one of those American oddball characters who washed up in California from New Jersey, moving in and out of a half-dozen obscure religious cults like British Israelism, based on the belief that the white population of Great Britain was directly descended from the Lost Tribes of Israel.

One of Swift's followers founded the militant organization known as Posse Comitatus in 1969. William Gale was a retired Army colonel living in Oregon, a part of the country that is to American militia movements what Liverpool was to British pop music. At a time when the federal government was using National Guard troops to enforce integration, members of Posse Comitatus refused to recognize any legal authority higher than a local sheriff, and if the group disagreed with the sheriff, their "Constitution" had a specific solution. "He shall be removed by the Posse to the most populated intersection of streets in the township and at high noon be hung by the neck, the body remaining until sundown as an example to those who would subvert the law."

If that sounds a lot like the "Hang Mike Pence" chant of the January 6 mob who brought a mock gallows to the Capitol grounds, it's no accident. The racist anti-government roots of the Posse Comitatus later merged with anti-tax and anti–gun control groups and morphed into what became known as the Sovereign Citizens movement. When an Iowa farm boy quit his job at John Deere and moved his family to an isolated corner of Northwest Idaho, he ran for sheriff with the slogan "Get Out Of Jail—Free," with the promise not to enforce any tax or gun laws. Randy Weaver was a white supremacist whose son and wife became martyrs for the anti-government movement when they were killed by federal agents trying to arrest Weaver on a warrant for violating gun laws. What became known as the "Siege of Ruby Ridge" served as the perfect rallying cry that united factions of anti-government groups across the country.

Weaver met a paid government informer working for the ATF at a gathering of the Aryan Nation in Idaho. The agent became friends with Weaver and asked for his help in procuring sawed-off shotguns. Weaver sold him two and said he could get more. That resulted in a warrant for his arrest, which set in motion a series of overreactions and blunders that killed Weaver's fourteen-year-old son and his wife. Like Ashli Babbitt, shot by a Capitol policeman guarding members of Congress on January 6, 2021, Vicki Weaver and her son became martyrs for the cause. "Nowhere was the horror of Ruby Ridge more acutely registered than in the white power movement," historian Kathleen Belew wrote in *Bring the War Home: The White Power Movement and Paramilitary America*, published by Harvard University Press. The infamous white supremacist Louis Beam wrote in the newsletter of the Aryan Nation, "The blood of these innocent ones, like a prism, makes everything clear. Ten thousand Randy Weavers are spread out from one coast to another."

Ruby Ridge was a law enforcement debacle. In testimony in front of a congressional inquiry, Weaver came across as a sympathetic family man who just wanted to be left alone by the government. He was awarded $3.1 million in compensation for the deaths of his son and wife, and the FBI agent who supervised the siege was suspended and then demoted.

That a guy selling a couple of illegal shotguns could end up with government agents killing his son and wife confirmed all the worst fears of anti-government conspirators, including a strange character in California who had recently changed his name from William Howell to David Koresh. A year later, federal agents would surround his Branch Davidian compound, and this time, 79 people would die, including 21 children. Two years later, a white separatist named Timothy McVeigh sought revenge for these deaths by blowing up the Murrah Federal Building in Oklahoma City. One hundred and sixty-eight were killed; 19 were children.

The Ruby Ridge siege was followed by the Branch Davidian siege, followed by the Oklahoma City bombing. Picture the events not as a series of isolated, tragic disasters but as a linked chain, each building on the previous. These are the Trinity of the Anti-Government Church. When Donald Trump holds a rally in Waco, Texas, he is gathering the communicants of the Church. What was once a fringe tragedy of American society with sad and damaged leading characters like Randy Weaver, David Koresh, and Tim McVeigh has become the largest faction of the Republican Party led by a former president of the United States.

Since 2015, when he announced his candidacy for president, the spectacle of Donald Trump's volcanic eruptions of anger and lies has inevitably conditioned much of the public and the media to ignore the specifics of his incendiary rhetoric. This is the phenomenon referenced in the previous chapter about Peter Thiel defending Trump with his oft-repeated construct that the media takes Trump literally but not seriously while the voters take him seriously but not literally. It is why Republican United States senators who knew Donald Trump had lost the 2020 race refused to condemn him for not accepting the results, reassuring each other's cowardice with "humor him, what harm can it do?" Weeks later when they were running for their lives in the Capitol, they had a better sense of the harm.

But even after Trump's violent rhetoric inspired the January 6 attack, there continues to be an inability to accept the continued danger he poses to American democracy. It's impossible to blame Donald Trump for this lack of alarm. He is doing everything possible to warn America but we still aren't listening. On the thirtieth anniversary of the Branch Davidian siege, Trump opened his presidential campaign in Waco with a call to arms: "Twenty twenty-four is the final battle," Trump declared. "If you put me back in the White House, their reign will be over, and America will be a free nation once again." This was unlike any announcement for a president in American history. Trump is not pretending to be participating in a democracy. His explicit and stated intent is to use the 2024 election to end democracy. The jackbooted thugs of the federal government may have won the day at Waco years ago, but we will get our revenge. "I am your warrior. I am your justice...I am your retribution. We will take care of it. We will take care of it."

Those who have dedicated their careers to studying hate movements and far-right extremism understand exactly what Trump is doing. "Waco is hugely symbolic on the far right," said Heidi Beirich, cofounder of the Global Project

Against Hate and Extremism, in a *USA Today* interview. "There's not really another place in the U.S. that you could pick that would tap into these deep veins of anti-government hatred—Christian nationalist skepticism of the government." After Waco, "the militia movement surged to more than 50,000 members in 47 states and focused increasingly on taking violent action to stop the rampant federal government," extremism historian Kathleen Belew wrote in her study of the white power movement, *Bring the War Home: The White Power Movement and Paramilitary America*.

The Trump announcement at Waco was a declaration of war against American democracy made to a well-armed crowd eager to be his soldiers. It was held in the shadow of a soon-to-be-announced indictment of Trump in New York for his role in the hush money payments to Stormy Daniels. Like Randy Weaver and David Koresh, Trump was a victim of an out-of-control Deep State conspiracy. "Let there be no doubt the injustice is being done, not only to me, but to dozens across our country and we're not going to stand for it." Trump was running to make it safe again for white Americans to claim their rightful place. "When this election is over, I will be the President of the United States. You will be vindicated and proud and the thugs and criminals who are corrupting our justice system will be defeated, discredited, and totally disgraced."

"He's being unjustly accused," Kathleen Belew described

in a *USA Today* interview, "like the Branch Davidians were unjustly accused—and the deep state is out to get them all."

Trump made it clear he has no use for the fundamental building block of any democracy, the willingness to lose. "Either the deep state destroys America, or we destroy the deep state."

Since Trump emerged, his appeal to white evangelicals has been a constant source of questions. How could these conservative Christians support a man who considers church that place you go to every ten years or so to marry a model? Like so much about Trump's appeal, there has been a need to search for some higher purpose that motivates those drawn to his anger and hate. Lost in the discussion of Trump's great appeal to evangelicals is the acknowledgment that it is white evangelicals who have flocked to Trump. Black evangelicals vote in large numbers opposed to Trump. This raises the obvious question: If white evangelicals love Trump and Black evangelicals hate him, is this about religion or race? And like all of Trump's appeals, it is about race.

White evangelicals are drawn to Trump as a socially accepted way to express their racially driven fears and anger. Trump's evocation of a "final battle" is deeply rooted in Christian nationalism. As Philip Gorski and Samuel Perry wrote in their 2022 book, *The Flag and the Cross*, as absurd as it might seem that a three-time divorced failed casino owner who bragged about grabbing women by the pussy could appeal to conservative Christians, Trump fits a narrative of white Christian nationalism:

> The first thing to note is that Trump's MAGA narrative can be understood as a semi-secularized version of white Christian nationalism's deep story. Trump's narrative is shorn of the sorts of biblical references and allusions that peppered earlier presidents' speeches. But the MAGA narrative still has many parallels with the deep story. The most obvious one is between the apocalyptic strand of white Christian nationalism and the catastrophizing aspect of MAGA. Premillennialists believe that there will be a final battle between good and evil, a life-and-death struggle between natural and supernatural forces that is visible to them, but invisible to unbelievers. Trump's worldview is similar. "Disaster" is one of his favorite words. He sees life as an endless battle between us and them. He sees hidden conspiracies everywhere he looks. We should not be surprised that Trump's rhetoric resonated so strongly with many white devotees of Christian nationalism. Their deep stories are quite similar.

In his Waco kickoff rally, Trump presented the choice in the 2024 presidential election not as a competition between two political parties but as a choice between good and evil.

"You're at a very pivotal point in our country," Trump told his followers. "Either we descend into a lawless abyss of open borders, rampant killings, super hyperinflation, which is what we have right now and not coming down, and festering corruption. Or we evict Joe Biden and the Democrats from the White House, and we make America great again." The "lawless abyss" evokes the pit of Hell, while "open borders" stoke the terror of a non-white nation.

Trump's success as a candidate of racial grievance is based on his authenticity. As Steve Bannon once said, "Dude, he's Archie Bunker." Which is only partially true. Like Trump, Bunker was a bigot from Queens, but he was capable of loving his family and expressing empathy. He moved through the world like a normal human being who came from a certain culture with distinct prejudices, but he was redeemable. That was the essence of the parable that Norman Lear was presenting to millions of Americans: Yes, we have our differences within our national family, but through love and understanding, we can work through them to a better place.

That's not Donald Trump. For him, life is a constant zero-sum dynamic: You win or you lose. He has a visceral connection to violent followers based on shared grievance and a conviction they are fighting for a cause that democracy has betrayed. For Trump and his shock troops, the classic societal goals of utilizing civil rights laws to provide a legal framework for racial reconciliation are an attack on white society's natural place in American life. In the 2020 campaign, well aware that most of his supporters are white and close to 70 percent live in suburbs, Trump launched an attack on suburban integration, trying to stoke the normal "there goes the neighborhood" fears. "People fight all of their lives to get into the suburbs and have a beautiful home," he said. "There will be no more low-income housing forced into the suburbs." This came after he canceled sections of the Fair Housing Act to encourage neighborhood diversification added during the Obama administration. "It's been hell for suburbia."

That was in 2020, but it tracks with decades of racist tendencies. In 1973, Donald Trump's name surfaced in the press for the first time when the Department of Justice sued the Trump Management Corporation—run by twenty-seven-year-old Donald Trump—for violating the Fair Housing Act. The DOJ charged Trump's company with a wide range of discriminatory actions, including refusing to rent to Black people, lying to Black applicants about the availability of apartments, and changing the terms on leases to Black tenants. Trump's response was a mirror of his presidential campaign, predicting a "massive fleeing from the city of not only our tenants but communities as a whole."

A young DOJ lawyer working on the case recalls what Trump told her when they were taking a coffee break during his deposition. "You know, you don't want to live with them either."

You know, you don't want to live with them either. That's what Randy Weaver believed when he moved to Ruby Ridge, not far from the Aryan Brotherhood compound. That's what Wesley Swift believed when he founded the Church of Jesus Christ—Christian. William Gale founded the Posse Comitatus outraged by the federal government using troops to enforce racial mixing in schools. David Koresh and his followers withdrew to their own all-white world because they didn't "want to live with them either."

Trump has no faith in the justice system determining guilt or innocence. When six Hispanic and Black teenagers were arrested in 1989 for the horrific rape of a woman jogging in Central Park, Trump took out a full-page ad in New York City newspapers. That ad stands as an extraordinarily self-revealing insight into the depths of cruelty and anger within Trump. It could have been written by any white supremacist desperate for retribution. It is a public appeal for a lynching, as illuminating about its author as *Mein Kampf*:

BRING BACK THE DEATH PENALTY. BRING BACK OUR POLICE!

...Mayor [Ed] Koch has stated that hate and rancor should be removed from our hearts. I do not think so. I want to hate these muggers and murderers. They should be forced to suffer and, when they kill, they should be executed for their crimes. They must serve as examples so that others will think long and hard before committing a crime or an act of violence. Yes, Mayor Koch, I want to hate these murderers and I always will. I am not looking to psychoanalyze them or understand them, I am looking to punish them. If the punishment is strong, the attacks on innocent people will stop. I recently watched a newscast trying to explain "the anger in these young men". I no longer want to understand their anger. I want them to understand our anger. I want them to be afraid....

CIVIL LIBERTIES END WHEN AN ATTACK ON OUR SAFETY BEGINS!

The five were later exonerated when convicted murderer Matias Reyes in 2002 confessed to the crime, confirmed by DNA evidence. As president, when asked if he would apologize for attacking innocent men, Trump gave the same response as when asked to condemn the neo-Nazi marchers in Charlottesville. "You have people on both sides of that," Trump said, insisting, "They admitted their guilt."

Trump's full-page ad called for the torture—"they should be made to suffer"—and execution of non-white men who had violated a white woman. There is no other way to say this than the simple truth: The Republican Party nominated, elected, and still supports a man who from the Oval

Office defended his calls for a public lynching of innocent Hispanic and Black teenagers.

"I think if Trump wins we could really legitimately say that he was associated directly with us, with the 'R' word [racist], all sorts of things," white supremacist Richard Spencer said shortly before the 2016 election. "People will have to recognize us."

Trump wasn't elected despite his anger and bigotry. The energy of that hate is what made him so appealing to most Republicans. It wasn't socially acceptable to say, "I like Trump because he hates Muslims," or "Trump is my guy because he calls Mexicans rapists," or "I want a president who will say there are good people who are neo-Nazis." Instead, it was phrased as "Trump tells it like it is," "finally somebody is making sense," and "he's not afraid to tell the truth." It is a constant of white supremacists to assert they have nothing against Black people. "We just want to be left alone" is a standard line of David Duke's, just as "I am the least racist person in the world" is a Trump refrain.

For most of American history, the structure of governance combined with the demographics of the country made it inevitable that whites would control the power centers of the country on every front: political, economic, educational, law enforcement, and judicial. Until a hundred years ago, it was only white men. There is nothing new about white political figures winning elections on a racist message. The first political race that I ever worked in was volunteering as a kid for William Winter's campaign for governor in Mississippi. He lost to the last openly segregationist governor in Mississippi, John Bell Williams.

What made Donald Trump's rise to power so shocking is that he emerged when most Americans would have assumed the country had moved beyond a time when an openly racist candidate could win national office. It is like Russia invading Ukraine in 2022. A land war of genocide in Europe? Didn't the civilized world agree that would never happen again?

But just as Vladimir Putin saw a successful democratic Ukraine as a great threat, Trump and his supporters believe the inevitable and accelerating changes in America are an existential threat to their survival. The use of violence to "save" their America is not only justified, it is a moral imperative.

There was a time when conservatives attacked liberals for "situational ethics," values that shifted when convenient. When I was active in the Republican Party, this was a standard trope. I'd like to say the hypocrisy of it troubled me, but it didn't. It was part of a useful collection of assumptions that allowed Republicans, myself included, to operate with the casual conviction that we were right and they were wrong. I say "casual" because the obviousness of these truths was so apparent, they required no more thought than wondering in which direction the sun might rise tomorrow. We were the party of Character Counts, Law and Order, Strong on Russia, Family Values.

None of it proved true, and nothing exposes the fraud more than the "Law and Order" party's embrace of violence. Donald Trump is not a political figure; he is Retribution Rambo, a superhero pulling open his business suit to reveal his true identity, eyes blazing with death rays. Republicans' need for a Strongman is so great, they have turned an obese old man in makeup into their violent masculine ideal. In a world threatened with chaos, the American right idolizes white men with guns who have the courage to stand up.

And who is it that these heroes are standing up to? Invariably the threat comes from Black people.

In a St. Louis suburb, a white lawyer and his wife became Republican heroes when they stood in their yard and waved guns at peaceful Black Lives Matter marchers. They were invited to speak to the 2016 Republican Convention, where, of course, they presented themselves as the true victims. "Not a single person in the out-of-control mob you saw at our house was charged with a crime. But you know who was? We were."

A wealthy white couple standing in front of their faux mansion with guns facing unarmed, peaceful protestors are not just protecting their own home but the homes of white people across America. "They want to abolish the suburbs altogether by ending single-family home zoning," Patricia McCloskey, the wife of the weapon-brandishing couple, warned; the Democrats "would bring crime, lawlessness, and low-quality apartments into thriving suburban neighborhoods."

A confused and troubled teenager named Kyle Rittenhouse has his mom drive him into another state with an AR-15 semiautomatic rifle to the site of protests following the shooting of an unarmed Black man that left him paralyzed. Rittenhouse says he was motivated to "act as a medic and observer," two roles traditionally performed without a semiautomatic weapon. A couple of hours later, he killed two men. A jury acquitted him of murder charges, and the young man is embraced by the right as a hero.

When a white police officer is convicted of murdering an unarmed Black man named George Floyd by kneeling on his neck for nine and a half minutes, former Fox News host Tucker Carlson calls the verdict "an attack on civilization." Right-wing blogger Matt Walsh tweeted, "A few years ago, George Floyd forced his way into a woman's home and robbed her at gunpoint. Today, that woman has to watch as millions turn her victimizer into their messiah. We are a sick country." Walsh, who later would ride his personal obsession with transgenderism into a lucrative business, tweeted, "The only systemic and institutional racism left in America is anti-white racism."

Calls for violence against those with whom you disagree have become completely normalized in the Republican Party. Florida Governor Ron DeSantis speaks longingly of wanting to assault Dr. Anthony Fauci, the man President George W. Bush awarded the Medal of Freedom in 2008 for his work saving millions in the AIDS epidemic.

"Someone needs to grab that little elf and chuck him across the Potomac," DeSantis said in one of his speeches setting the table for his presidential run.

Like Donald Trump and Putin, physical size is a particularly sensitive subject with DeSantis, who is fond of boots with heels high enough to make any stripper jealous. In the first video ad for his 2024 presidential race, his campaign presents him as the new Savior, announcing in a deep God-like voice: "And on the eighth day, God looked down on his planned paradise and said: 'I need a protector.' So God made a fighter." God is mentioned ten times in the ninety-second ad in what advertising executives would call prime "product placement."

Never Back Down is the name of the super PAC supporting the Ron DeSantis campaign for president. The name is intended to evoke the Strongman persona Republicans covet. To bolster his authoritarian image, DeSantis picked a fight with Disney when the company refused to embrace DeSantis's anti-gay legislation. When DeSantis threatened to build a state prison next to Disney World to prove who was really boss, the company promptly canceled a billion-dollar expansion planned for Florida, which would have brought thousands of high-paying jobs to the state. Once, the Republican Party was Ronald Reagan standing in front of the Berlin Wall challenging, "Mr. Gorbachev, tear down this wall." Now it's Ron DeSantis whining in front of the Magic Kingdom, calling Mickey Mouse out for a fight. And then losing the fight.

Violence has become an essential element of the Republican political narrative, signaling to the once fringe militia groups and their sympathizers that they have a place in the party. When once it would have been bizarre for a candidate to appear in a campaign ad firing a high-caliber weapon, it is now a standard trope, no less expected than marching in a Fourth of July parade. (I can say with at least a touch of pride that while there is much I regret about the years I spent in the Republican Party, of the thousands of ads I made over thirty years, never did I film a candidate firing a deadly weapon.) While it is often cached as a proof point of the candidate's support of the Second Amendment, this is information the intended audience assumes. There are no Republican candidates running who are not supporters of the Second Amendment. Its real purpose is to bond with the large segment of the candidate's voter base that views the election not as a political contest but a potential referendum for a race war.

The Republican Party has evolved from a party that passively accepted the support of militia groups and their kindred spirits into assuming the role of the elected representatives of America's violent anti-government factions. To rise in the Republican Party, it is essential to show solidarity with those who wish to end democracy.

This is why an ambitious young politician like Senator Josh

Hawley of Missouri parades in front of the January 6 insurrectionists with a raised fist. Hawley is a prep school grad who went to Stanford, taught at St. Paul's in London, graduated from Yale Law School, and wrote a biography of Teddy Roosevelt published by Yale Press. In a functioning, governing political party, he would be a stabilizing voice of reason, drawing on his education at America's finest institutions to help his country. This was the role played by his predecessor Senator John Danforth from 1976 until 1995, a Republican who, like Hawley, went to elite schools, Princeton and Yale Law School, and, like Hawley, was first elected attorney general of Missouri. Heir to the Ralston Purina fortune, Danforth was an ordained Episcopal minister, who wrote a 2005 Op-Ed piece in the *New York Times* that warned, "By a series of recent initiatives, Republicans have transformed our party into the political arm of conservative Christians." He had supported his fellow Yale Law graduate Hawley when he ran for the Senate and later called it "the biggest mistake of my life."

After he demonstrated his solidarity with the gathering mob at the Capitol by raising his fist, a couple of hours later, Hawley was captured on video running for his life from the same mob. Once he had escaped, Hawley returned to the Senate floor to end the democratic transference of power by voting not to certify the election results.

Like the paramilitary groups attacking the Capitol, Hawley is both a symbol and a cause of a deteriorating democratic state. You do not assault the Capitol unless you believe the democratic process has failed and must end. You do not refuse to certify the election of the candidate who received more votes than any presidential candidate in U.S. history if you respect the will of the people, an essential element for any democracy to survive. Both the insurrectionists and the senator from Missouri are representatives of the large and growing group of Americans who doubt the legitimacy and efficacy of the elected government.

In his famous 1919 essay "Politics as a Vocation," German sociologist Max Weber defined the state as "the form of human community that (successfully) lays claim to the monopoly of legitimate physical violence." This is the fundamental principle that the dominant MAGA elements of the Republican Party have abandoned. They attack the very foundations of a civil society, the judiciary and law enforcement, because they are unwilling to accept the premise that a state exists for a greater good that might conflict with what they perceive as their own good. The far right is obsessed with guns and violence because they reject what Weber rightly articulated as the essence of a shared community. "For what is specific to the present," Weber wrote, "is that all other organizations or individuals can assert the right to use physical violence only insofar as the state permits them to do so. The state is regarded as the sole source of the 'right' to use violence."

That is a concept that Republicans now fundamentally reject. They have convinced themselves that they live in a dark and dangerous world under constant threat. Walking into a Starbucks with a semiautomatic weapon isn't proving you have the right to bear arms; it is an assertion that you do not trust society to protect you, that there is no civil bond between you and the next person in line ordering a latte. You have lost faith in a government to bring order, and you fear the government for its power to take away your gun, which is the only source of security in which you have confidence.

There is a growing sense of the inevitability of violence in America, which acts as an accelerant for more violence. If society accepts that it is impossible to control guns, it becomes logical that the only solution is more guns. If we accept that school shootings are beyond the reach of a governmental solution, then the only protection from violence becomes more violence. While other Western democracies focus on putting computers in every classroom, America is putting guns in every classroom, arming teachers and school administrators. Surrounding children with armed protection is how drug lords try to protect their children, not a functioning democracy. It is difficult to imagine a more powerful symbol of a failed society than one that cannot protect its youngest and most vulnerable.

As the Republican Party increasingly has become the political arm of a vastly corrupt National Rifle Association,

America has been conducting a social experiment on the impact of a major party normalizing violence as part of the political process. It was perfectly acceptable to the Republican Party when Donald Trump called out to the domestic terrorist group the Proud Boys in a debate, telling them "to stand back and stand by." Trump routinely uses QAnon conspiracy language and symbolism, such as "The Storm Is Coming," and has played the QAnon song "WWG1WGA" ("Where we go one, we go all") at rallies. In classic autocratic style, intimidation by violence is used to enforce loyalty to the autocrat. In a profile of thirty-four-year-old Michigan Republican Congressman Peter Meijer in *The Atlantic*, Tim Alberta describes the scene as the House of Representatives was voting on certification of the election on January 6, 2021:

> On the House floor, moments before the vote, Meijer approached a member who appeared on the verge of a breakdown. He asked his new colleague if he was okay. The member responded that he was not; that no matter his belief in the legitimacy of the election, he could no longer vote to certify the results, because he feared for his family's safety. "Remember, this wasn't a hypothetical. You were casting that vote after seeing with your own two eyes what some of these people are capable of," Meijer says. "If they're

willing to come after you inside the U.S. Capitol, what will they do when you're at home with your kids?"

Liz Cheney described to CNN the impact of fear on her Republican colleagues: "If you look at the vote to impeach, for example, there were members who told me that they were afraid for their own security—afraid, in some instances, for their lives. And that tells you something about where we are as a country, that members of Congress aren't able to cast votes, or feel that they can't, because of their own security."

In Cheney's last unsuccessful race in Wyoming, her campaign spent tens of thousands of dollars on security and she was forced to limit her campaign appearances. Trump repeatedly targeted her. "Liz Cheney is a bitter, horrible human," Trump said after she was ousted from party leadership before her defeat. "I watched her yesterday and realized how bad she is for the Republican Party."

In healthy democracies, the heads of state act as a calming influence, reassuring citizens that their safety is protected by the governmental policies and institutions of the state. Dictators act in exactly the opposite manner, constantly churning the fears of a populace so that their only hope of security lies with the brutal acts of a Strongman. Ruth Ben-Ghiat describes it perfectly in her *Strongmen: Mussolini to the Present*:

From the start, authoritarians stand out from other kinds of politicians by appealing to negative experiences and emotions. They don the cloak of national victimhood, reliving the humiliations of their people by foreign powers as they proclaim themselves their nation's saviors. Picking up on powerful resentments, hopes, and fears, they present themselves as the vehicle for obtaining what is most wanted, whether it is territory, safety from racial others, securing male authority, or payback for exploitation by internal or external enemies.

When Trump declares, "I alone can fix it," he is telling his followers that their government has failed. It establishes the precedent for violent action by nongovernmental actors. In a society with a nonfunctioning government, it is not a terrorist act to take up arms to protect what and whom you love. Forming a militia to protect your community then becomes an act of responsibility, not revolution. America began when patriots rose to defend their rights. The Three Percenters explicitly see themselves as the heirs to the small numbers of brave men who took a stand against tyranny. Of course, their history is wrong, and the actual numbers were far higher, but these men who resemble the guys working at Home Depot in body armor are about the business of saving the country, not passing AP History.

The day Trump announced his candidacy for president in 2015, calling Mexicans "rapists," it was impossible to predict that on January 6, 2021, an armed mob would storm the Capitol in an attempt to overturn election results. When Trump rallies became a festival of violence, with Trump threatening the press—"enemies of the people"—and urging his supporters to beat up protestors—"knock the crap out of them. I'll pay the legal bills"—there was no way of knowing that he would become the first defeated president to refuse to accept election results and would succeed in convincing the majority of his party that America did not have a legal president.

When Donald Trump calls his campaign to return to the White House "the final battle," no one can say where this will lead.

When the governor of Florida announced he will refuse to obey a court order and not allow New York to extradite Donald Trump from Florida, who can predict what a state rejecting the laws of another might mean? Did anyone know in March 1857 that the *Dred Scott* decision would be settled with a civil war, not court orders?

But what do we know? We know that today for the first time since the 1860s, a major American political party has refused to accept that a president was legally elected. We know that a president's party refused to convict on Articles of Impeachment after he led a rebellion that attempted to murder the second highest member of the U.S. government and their own colleagues. We know that the man whom polling shows is currently defeating the incumbent president of the United States has pledged to pardon those who were convicted for their role in an effort to overthrow the government of the United States. We know that man is running not to govern but for "retribution."

So we actually do know a great deal. A man who explicitly called for armed followers to help him stay in power is on track to return to power. We know that no anti-democratic movement became more democratic once in power. We know that America is caught in an ever-escalating cycle of violence that hangs over our society like the threat of nuclear war did for a previous generation. The "duck and cover" drills of the Cold War have been replaced with active shooter drills that teach students to throw schoolbooks at semiautomatic weapons. Parents must warn their children that knocking on a stranger's door to ask for directions may end in their murder. We know that even our nation's highest leaders are fearful of the state security apparatus intended to serve as their protection. "I'm not getting in that car," Vice President Pence told his Secret Service detail.

A nation with more guns than citizens in which the majority of one party believes there is an illegal occupant as head of state, where those who deny election results are rewarded, is not a stable democracy. There are two likely scenarios for the 2024 election: (1) Donald Trump or a Trumpist surrogate will win the Republican nomination and be elected president. Or (2) Donald Trump or a Trumpist surrogate will win the Republican nomination and Joe Biden will be re-elected.

Under the first scenario, America will rapidly accelerate toward the autocracy of Hungary that Republicans so admire. Under the second, the defeated Trumpist candidate will refuse to accept the results, and January 6, 2021, will look like the bloodless Fort Sumter engagement compared to what followed.

The collapse of American democracy is like the pandemic: Whatever you say at the beginning will sound alarmist but likely prove inadequate by the end. In 1864, Lincoln wrote, "You cannot escape the responsibility of tomorrow by evading it today." We should listen and act accordingly.

Driving Toward Autocracy

In the years I worked in politics, I was always the optimist, the guy who thought that no matter how far down we might be in a race, we could still win. Down ten points with three days to go? Not a problem. The solution is out there, the perfect closing message, the better argument. We can do this.

I didn't always win, but I won a lot more than I lost, and along the way, I became a believer in the power of believing. I was the Ted Lasso "Believe" guy, and it served me well.

Today I find myself in a strange and uncomfortable position. Somewhere along the way, I had a going-out-of-business sale for any optimism I could manage for the Republican Party.

I don't want to be this person. There is a joy and energy to optimism, a shared compact with a future of opportunity and hope, which I deeply miss.

It's not really the Republican Party I am worried about; it's what the party is doing to America. Trump and Trumpism are as pure evil as has existed in mainstream politics, and when I look around, I, too, often see the institutions of America failing the moment. It doesn't come in the active embrace of Trumpism but in a failure aggressively and unequivocally to reject an authoritarian movement of hate. My fear is that America is learning to accommodate Trumpism, and history is clear that is a gateway drug to democratic collapse.

Why is it that CNN even considered rebranding as the network that would tell both sides when one side is a palace of lies that calls journalists "the enemy of the people"? Why is it that CBS finds it acceptable to hire a former Trump White House chief of staff, Mick Mulvaney, who eagerly defended Trump's lies and promoted the COVID policy that helped kill hundreds of thousands of Americans?

So you can be part of that and just walk away without consequences? Worse, walk away and be rewarded for your participation in evil?

Today Ron DeSantis is embraced by many of what passes for a conservative intelligentsia who found Trump distasteful. Ron DeSantis? A man who advocates the power of the state to ban books, punish businesses who disagree, and create a private police force to intimidate voters? Ron DeSantis, who agrees with Vladimir Putin that Russia's war of genocide is a "territorial dispute"? Really? That's what conservatism has come to?

Because DeSantis is better educated than Trump and has never bragged about assaulting women, he's now a conservative savior? Being a little more socially acceptable than Trump now makes you the next Ronald Reagan?

What Patrick Moynihan called "defining deviancy down" is too often becoming the acceptable standard for political decency.

If I am depressed, it's because it's depressing. Watching my old party is like seeing an alcoholic drink himself to death and shatter a family.

———

I'm often asked what would be a sign that the Republican Party has a desire to change, to return to the American family of governing political parties? There's the obvious answer if a candidate emerged who actively ran against Trumpism and won. Someone who had never bent the knee to Trump and was clearly motivated by principle. That's not going to happen in 2024, and as much as I'd like to believe otherwise, it isn't going to happen in 2028. But a hopeful first step would be if the party could join the reality-based world and admit, if not assert, that Donald Trump lost a free and fair election in 2020. Until then, it will continue to have the same position of Russia, North Korea, and Iran that America isn't really a functioning democracy.

For thirty years, I pointed out flaws in the Democratic Party. I'm sure if I looked back, some of that criticism would stand as valid and some as partisan bullshit, but there is always a lot of partisan bullshit in campaigns. None of that matters now. The inescapable truth is that there is now only one pro-democratic party in American politics, and that's the Democratic Party. The Republican Party has proven there is no line that can be crossed, no principle shattered, that will force the party to return to decency. If you are unwilling to hold the man accountable who sent a mob to kill you and your colleagues, what other possible transgression could merit a response?

Pain is the best teacher in politics. The Republican Party is like the Russian state: The only way it will leave Ukraine is if defeated. There is no negotiation that is not based on delusion. The only hope for the Republican Party is for it to suffer crushing defeat after crushing defeat so that it is forced to confront its failure. Then maybe, just maybe, it will begin to change and return to some semblance of a normal center-right party in a democratic civil society.

This means that the only way to move forward with the possibility of two sane parties in America is to vote for Democratic candidates. Not voting or casting a protest vote is a vote for Trumpism. I have friends who tell me quite smugly that they refused to vote for Trump but voted for Mike Pence. How does that work? It's childish at a moment when our nation is crying out for honest adults.

There is no national solution to this national crisis. It is up to each of us individually to do what it takes to save the

America we love. We are our own last best hope. No one is coming to save us. We are our own destiny.

Maybe I still do believe. America is so much more than a place on a map with a flag. We must fight not because we know we will emerge triumphant but fight because not to fight is to give up. And if we do that, we no longer deserve to call ourselves Americans.

Acknowledgments

A special note of deep appreciation to Velda Fayz, whose research skills and general smarts were invaluable as I wrote *Conspiracy*. Eileen Klomhaus, Sarah Banks, and Dylan Croll were a great help with research, sourcing, and ideas. As he was with my last book, Scott Merriman was always there to help as a reader and researcher.

Russell Martin, my friend since college, helped guide the book from conception to completion, bringing his immense talents as a writer, reader, and editor.

Reid Singer was extraordinarily helpful in the fact-checking and research for *Conspiracy*.

As always, any errors and mistakes are completely my fault and responsibility.

About the Author

Stuart Stevens is the author of eight previous books, most recently, the bestselling *It Was All a Lie*, and his work has appeared in the *New York Times*, the *Washington Post*, *Esquire*, and *Outside*, among other publications. He has written extensively for television shows, including *Northern Exposure*, *Commander in Chief*, and *K Street*. For twenty-five years, he was the lead strategist and media consultant for some of the nation's toughest political campaigns.